Batsford Chess Library

Winning Moves 2

Raymond Keene

An Owl Book
Henry Holt and Company
New York

Henry Holt and Company, Inc.
Publishers since 1866
115 West 18th Street
New York, New York 10011

Henry Holt® is a registered
trademark of Henry Holt and Company, Inc.

Published in Canada by Fitzhenry & Whiteside Ltd.,
195 Allstate Parkway, Markham, Ontario L3R 4T8.
First published in the United States in 1996 by
Henry Holt and Company, Inc.
Originally published in Great Britain in 1996 by
B. T. Batsford Ltd.

Library of Congress Catalog Card Number: 95-81556

ISBN 0-8050-8155-6 (An Owl Book: pbk.)

First American Edition - 1996

Printed in the United Kingdom
All first editions are printed on acid-free paper. ∞

10   9   8   7   6   5   4   3   2   1

To the Games Gurus Alex and Gertrude Randolph

Editorial Panel: Mark Dvoretsky, John Nunn, Jon Speelman
General Adviser: Raymond Keene OBE
Commissioning Editor: Graham Burgess

Contents

Introduction

This is the second book based on the Winning Move puzzles which appear every day in *The Times*, and for which every week prizes are offered for correct solutions. The positions may simply be enjoyed for the intellectual challenge that they offer, but they may also serve as a tool for sharpening the tactical ability of the reader, thus improving his or her ability to spot winning moves in actual play. Finally, the puzzles in the book have been constructed so as to offer the reader a progressive grading system both for each chapter and for the book as a whole. Every position offers points to be scored and at the end of each chapter the reader will be offered the opportunity to add up the points scored and assess his or her level of strength. It is to be hoped that this level will improve as the reader becomes more experienced by delving further into the book. By adding up the points scored in each chapter and consulting the chapter on ratings the reader will gain a good overall perspective of the general playing standard attained. The points scored indicate level of strength, i.e. rating and category of player (grandmaster, master, expert etc.).

The Times Winning Move puzzle has helped *The Times* to gain the largest circulation of readers amongst chessplayers. Each year the British Chess Problem Society issues a prize chess puzzle which they request all papers with chess columns to publish. The reader response rate for this is widely accepted as the most accurate barometer of which newspapers are being most popularly read for chess. In 1995 BCPS officials who run the competition announced that *The Times* had yet again won the award for the greatest reader response. The winning percentage for *The Times* was also dominant.

	Publication	Reader Response (%)
1	*The Times*	58.02%
2	*Mail on Sunday*	11.87%
3	*The Guardian*	9.89%
4	*Sunday Telegraph*	7.91%
5	*Daily Telegraph*	5.71%
6	*Financial Times*	4.40%
7	*Evening Standard*	2.20%

Good luck with the solving.

Raymond Keene, *Times* Chess Correspondent

How to Follow the Chess Moves

Chess, in distinction to almost all other sports, has a perfect medium in algebraic notation for reliving the drama and details of any specific game. Readers who are comparatively new to the game, or who have only learned the older 'English Descriptive' notation, will find what follows helpful. It is assumed that the reader has progressed beyond the absolute beginner level and already knows how to play chess.

In writing down the moves, each piece is represented by a figurine as follows:

Knight	♞	or	N
Bishop	♝	or	B
Rook	♜	or	R
Queen	♛	or	Q
King	♚	or	K

We do not customarily use a special symbol for pawns when writing down the moves.

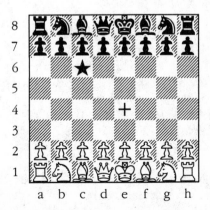

The squares on the chessboard are described by co-ordinates, consisting of a letter followed by a number (see diagram). For instance the square marked with a cross is called 'e4', the square marked with a star is called 'c6'. This follows exactly the same principle as reading off a reference on an A-Z street guide or road map. Everybody can pick this up in a matter of minutes. There is no mystery to it at all.

Whenever a piece moves, the initial symbol of that piece appears at the start of the move. For example, White's fifth move in the following game shows that a knight (♘) moves to the square c3. When a pawn moves, only the square on which it arrives, when the move is completed, is mentioned. A perfect example is White's first move 1 e4 (white pawn goes to e4) in the game which follows and Black's first move 1...c5 (black pawn goes to c5). Captures are denoted by an 'x'. Thus Black's third move in the game 3...cxd4, shows that Black's pawn on the c-file captures White's pawn on d4.

Note also the following special symbols:

...	=	move by Black, standing on its own
!	=	strong move
?	=	mistake
+	=	check
0-0	=	castles kingside
0-0-0	=	castles queenside

A Quick Win
The following miniature game shows the algebraic system of chess notation in action. I have deliberately chosen a short game to make the introduction as easy as possible.

Ljubojevic - Kramnik
Belgrade 1995
Sicilian Defence

1 e4 c5 2 ♘f3 ♘c6 3 d4 cxd4 4 ♘xd4 ♘f6 5 ♘c3 e5 6 ♘db5 d6 7 ♗g5 a6 8 ♘a3 b5 9 ♗xf6 gxf6 10 ♘d5 ♗g7 11 g3 f5 12 exf5 e4 13 f6 ♗xf6 14 ♘xf6+ ♛xf6 15 ♛d5 0-0 16 c3 b4 17 ♘c4 bxc3 18 ♛xd6 ♗e6 19 ♛f4 ♛g7 20 0-0-0 ♘b4 21 ♛e5 ♘xa2+ 22 ♚b1 ♛xe5 23 ♘xe5 ♗b3 0-1

Here is a diagram showing the final position where White resigned. If White saves his attacked rook then the decisive ...c2+ will follow.

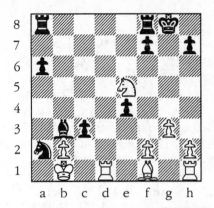

You cannot hope to win regularly if you do not know what the pieces are worth, and the value of the pieces is determined precisely by their respective mobility on an open board. **It is a golden rule of chess that most chess games are decided by extra material.** Even at beginner's level, the loss of a piece without compensation can result in the loss of the game. In master and grandmaster games the unplanned loss of even a single pawn is usually totally disastrous.

Here is a point count table to help you remember the relative strengths of the pieces.

♙	pawn	1 point
♘	knight	3 points
♗	bishop	3 points
♖	rook	5 points
♕	queen	9 points

This must be committed to memory.

Naturally, this table gives no value for the king (♔) since the object of chess is to give checkmate against the opposing king. Therefore, the king can never be exchanged or taken. If you like, the king is worth an infinite number of points, but as a fighting unit in the endgame it has about the same strength as a bishop or a knight.

Chess Ratings

Spaced throughout *The Times Winning Moves II* are six progressively more difficult, carefully graded, self-ranking tests, designed to give you, the reader, an idea of your potential chess ranking. Governing bodies, such as the PCA (the Professional Chess Association), FIDE (the World Chess Federation), the USCF (United States Chess Federation) and the BCF (British Chess Federation) regularly publish numerical ranking lists, giving the specific ratings of the strongest players. You may not qualify for that accolade just yet, but by completing the six tests successfully, you will be able to gain a clearer idea of how you shape up in the overall pantheon of chess. Do not be discouraged by an initially low rating - even if you score 1000 so-called Elo (World and US Chess Federation) points (equivalent to a British Chess Federation rating of 50) you will still be able to spot checkmate and win games. Indeed, a rating of 50 is equivalent to a White Belt in judo, something to be proud of, if you are just setting out on your playing career! By the way, it is worth pointing out that a rating of 2000 will be equivalent to a Black Belt First Dan in judo!

First of all, let us look at some of the top rankings in chess - mental Everests to which one can aspire.

Explanation of Chess Titles and Ratings
In order to acquire the title of international master or grandmaster, a player must achieve results (known as norms) in international competitions. The number of points required for a norm in any one event is calculated on the basis of the strength of the opposition in the tournament. For example, in a very strong tournament it may only be necessary to score 5/9 to achieve a grandmaster norm, whereas in a weaker tournament, a score of 7/9 might be the target. Usually, three norms are required for a title. For those who are new to chess ratings a regular ranking list is issued by the World Chess Federation. It was devised by Professor Arpad Elo. On Professor Elo's scale the following numbers correspond to the following playing strengths.

2815	Garry Kasparov (World Record Rating)
2700+	World Championship Candidate level
2600	Strong Grandmaster
2500	Grandmaster
2400	International Master
2300	FIDE Master
2200	US Life Master
2000	International FIDE-rated player

There follow some fascinating figures, showing some of the peak Elo ratings throughout the history of chess.

Elo Numbers

1	Kasparov	2815
2	Fischer	2785
3	Kramnik	2775
4	Karpov	2770
5	Kamsky	2741
6	Anand	2736
7	Ivanchuk	2735
8	Capablanca	2725
9	Lasker	2720
10	Botvinnik	2720
11	Shirov	2710
12=	Morphy, Alekhine	2690

Although these ratings are 'official' numbers, the inflation in ratings recently means that the old masters, Capablanca, Lasker and Botvinnik, have been slightly disadvantaged. I would personally place Capablanca, Lasker and Botvinnik at numbers 4, 5 and 6 just behind Kasparov, Fischer and Karpov. The young Russian grandmaster Vladimir Kramnik has made a sudden entry to the highest echelons of the list, achieving an extraordinary 2775 rating. It remains to be seen whether this is a flash in the pan or whether it is the first sign that a new great player is joining the all-time elite.

Now let us examine the range of ratings covered by the tests in this book. There are six chapters in all, covering the following scores.

Chapter 1 measures your potential up to 1000 Elo (international or US rating points) or 50 BCF (British Chess Federation). If you can score 1000 you are successfully commencing your chess career.

Chapter 2 measures your potential up to 1200 Elo or 75 BCF. If you score 1200 you are an experienced social player.

Chapter 3 measures your potential up to 1400 Elo or 100 BCF. If you score 1400 you have the ability to challenge your home computer.

Chapter 4 measures your potential up to 1600 Elo or 125 BCF. If you score 1600 you are of club player standard.

Chapter 5 measures your potential up to 1800 Elo or 150 BCF. If you score 1800 you are a strong club player or able to represent your region.

Chapter 6 measures your potential up to 2000 Elo or 175 BCF. If you score 2000 you are of international rating standard and capable of achieving a published international rating.

Chapter One

Starting Out - Up to 1,000
Try to answer all the puzzles. Award yourself 25 Elo points for each correct answer and a bonus of 5 Elo points if you solve the puzzle in less than three minutes. If you score 1000 points (e.g. you correctly solve all the positions without gaining any time bonuses), you can clearly be confident that you have successfully started on your chess career. If you score less than 1000, review the answers which caused you difficulty carefully before proceeding on the next test.

I strongly suggest that you write down your solution to all positions on a separate sheet of paper and check them out once you have completed the chapter. Otherwise the danger exists that you will inadvertently spot solutions to later positions when checking out the answers. Alternatively, if you wish to discover the answer to each position immediately after you have solved it, I recommend you use a sheet of paper to cover subsequent answers on the page while checking the solution. The answers to chapter one start on page 24.

1) White to play
This is a variation from Staunton - Worrall, London 1859. How could White exploit the power of his bishop pair in dramatic fashion?

3) White to play
Nunn - Murshed, London 1985. 1 ♖xe5 is a very strong move for White and, in fact, delivers mate in four moves. However, White actually has a way to mate even more quickly. Can you see it?

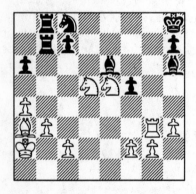

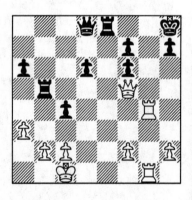

2) White to play
Nunn - Williams, Neath 1985. John Nunn is one of Britain's greatest attacking players. This position and the next two celebrate his attacking genius. How does White exploit this to deliver a quick mate?

4) White to play
Nunn - Pritchett, Bundesliga 1985.
White has broken through on the kingside. How does he deliver the *coup de grâce* with a checkmating combination?

5) White to play
Brynell - Dysing, Stockholm
1995.
White has a powerful attack on
the open g-file. How did he now
capitalise with a fine sacrifice?

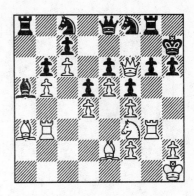

7) White to play
Glek - Kersetz, Bad Godesberg
1995.
White has gained space all over
the board and now needs to
open a line on the kingside to
finish off the game. How did he
achieve this with a neat tactic?

6) Black to play
Enqvist - Krasenkov, Stock-
holm 1995.
Black has many threats to cope
with: ♕xc8+, ♘xg3 and ♘f6+.
Can you see what he did?

8) White to play
de Firmian - Burgess, Gausdal
1995.
Here White would like to win
the black queen with 1 ♗h6+
♕xh6 2 ♖xh6, but then he loses
his own to 2...♖xa4. How can
he improve on this variation?

9) White to play
Sokolov - Oudeweetering, Holland 1995.
White is behind on material, but his tremendous pressure against the kingside is enough compensation. How does he now make the most of this?

11) Black to play
Meyers - Razuvaev, Berne 1995.
Material is level in this endgame, but the constricted position of the white king gives Black the chance for an immediate win. Can you spot it?

10) White to play
Ashley - Zso. Polgar, Bermuda 1995.
Here White played 1 ♕xg7+ and went on to win. However, he missed something much more terminal. What should he have played instead?

12) White to play
Kelecevic - Freiburghaus, Berne 1995.
In this equal-looking position White spotted the opportunity for a decisive breakthrough. What did he play?

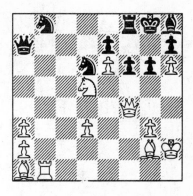

13) Black to play
Lautier - Illescas, Linares 1995.
In this innocent-looking end-game, White has just carelessly placed his knight on a5. How did Black now expose this as a bad blunder?

15) White to play
Mestrovic - Payen, Cannes 1995.
How did White finish off the game by spotting a neat tactical opportunity?

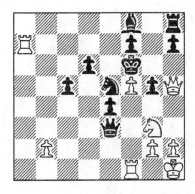

14) White to play
This is a variation from the game Burgess - Whitcutt, Torbay 1989.
The black king has been driven into the open. How does White now land the decisive blow?

16) White to play
Schone - Vigh, Budapest 1995.
Black has just moved his bishop to e5 to threaten the white queen. How did White demonstrate that this was a bad mistake?

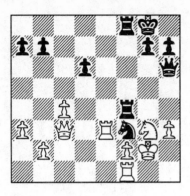

17) White to play
Toth - Szigetti, Budapest 1946.
White has given up a piece to open the h-file against the black king. However, his efforts are currently being impeded by the black queen. How did he overcome this problem?

19) Black to play
Holland - Shaw, London 1995.
Of the three pawns that defend a kingside castled position the g-pawn is usually the most valuable. Here, White has lost this pawn and now pays the ultimate price. How did Black continue?

18) White to play
This is a variation from the game Kramnik - Piket, Monaco 1995.
This is a position that has confused at least one international master. What is White's quickest win?

20) Black to play
Yusupov - Kasparov, Riga 1995.
World champion Kasparov here found a quiet move which quickly gained a decisive material advantage. What did he play?

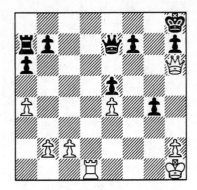

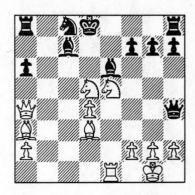

21) White to play
Oll - Cvitan, Belgium 1995.
White has a very active position for his sacrificed pawn but he must act quickly before Black can consolidate with ...♖a8. can you spot White's best continuation?

23) White to play
Blackburne - Smith, Brighton 1882.
With the black king trapped, in the centre, White has a fierce attack. Can you spot his immediate kill?

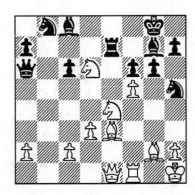

22) White to play
Littlewood - Hunt, Four Nations Chess League 1995.
How did White swiftly make a decisive material gain?

24) White to play
Wilson - Wright, Brighton 1893.
White has sacrificed a piece to open up the black king's defences. How did he now finish off with an accurate sequence?

25) White to play
Erskine - Wilson, Brighton
1890.
Snap checkmates are usually a
feature of complex middle-
games but this position sees one
in an endgame. How did White
force a quick mate?

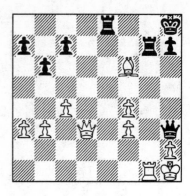

27) Black to play
Uhlmann - Dely, Budapest
1962.
Black, who is suffering from an
uncomfortable pin against his
rook on g7, appears to be in
trouble. How did he demonstrate that this was not the case?

26) White to play
Shoosmith - Ward, Tunbridge
Wells 1908.
How did Mr. Shoosmith, playing White, succeed in kicking
his way through his opponent's
kingside defences?

28) Black to play
Hansen - Müller, Denmark
1962.
Although Black is the exchange
(rook for bishop) down, he has
a very powerfully placed bishop
on e4. How did he make the
most of this?

29) White to play
Santo-Roman - Heurtebize,
France 1995.
How did White force a quick
checkmate?

31) White to play
Short - Kramnik, Novgorod
1995.
Black has just blundered, allowing White the chance for a
quick finish. What did he play?

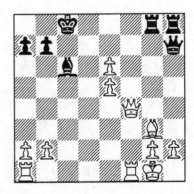

30) Black to play
Quadrio - Santos, Lisbon 1995.
The open g- and h-files give
Black promising attacking
prospects against the white
king. How did he make the
most of these?

32) Black to play
Hartikainen - Lyrberg, Gausdal
1994.
Black could win a pawn here by
capturing on d4. However, he
found something much stronger.
What did he play?

33) White to play
Here is a variation from a game from the Lasker - Steinitz, World Championship of 1896. The black forces are a long way from the scene of the action. How does White win immediately?

35) White to play
Capablanca - Lasker, World Championship 1921.
The great Cuban Capablanca was renowned for his almost flawless technical play but here he demonstrates his sharp tactical ability.

34) White to play
Lasker - Steinitz, World Championship 1894.
White is a piece down, but the black king is dangerously exposed. How did White continue?

36) Black to play
This is a variation from the game Capablanca - Alekhine, World Championship 1927.
The presence of four queens on the board creates unusual tactical possibilities. How did Alekhine utilise these?

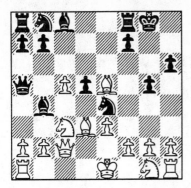

37) Black to play
Kasparov - Short, *Times* World Championship, London, game 5 1993.
White has just developed his bishop to d3. Would Black be well advised to continue with 1...♘xc3?

39) Black to play
Reiner - Steinitz, Vienna 1860. This is a typical 19th century position where White has grabbed material at the expense of his development. How did Black now punish him for his greed?

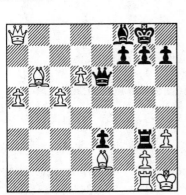

38) Black to play
This is a variation from Anand - Kasparov, Intel World Championship, Game 9 1995.
This position, which Anand easily avoided, demonstrates a last ditch try by Kasparov to turn the tables.

40) White to play
This position is a variation from Larsen - Kosten, Hastings Premier 1990.
Black is material ahead and appears to have a dangerous attack. However, it is White to play and he has a quick kill.

Solutions

1) 1 ♕xf6! gxf6 2 ♗xf6 mate.

2) 1 ♘f7+! ♗xf7 2 ♗b2+ ♗g7 3 ♗xg7+ ♔g8 4 ♘f6 mate.

3) 1 ♕g7+! ♗xg7 2 ♖xe8+ ♗f8 3 ♖xf8 mate.

4) 1 ♕xh7+! ♔xh7 2 ♖h4 mating.

5) 1 ♕xf7+! ♔xf7 2 ♖xg7 mate.

6) 1...♖g2+! 2 ♔xg2 ♘e3+ winning the white queen.

7) 1 ♘g5+! hxg5 2 ♖h3 mate.

8) 1 ♕xb5! and if 1...♕xb5 2 ♗h6+ ♔e8 3 ♖g8 is mate.

9) 1 ♖d7! wins, as if 1...♗xd7 2 ♕xg7 is mate.

10) 1 ♖xd6 wins on the spot, as 1...♕xd6 2 ♕xg7 is mate.

11) 1...♖h1+! 2 ♔xh1 ♖f1 mate.

12) 1 ♕xf5+! is decisive, as if 1...♔xf5 2 ♗d3 is mate.

13) 1...♘xe2 2 ♔xe2 ♗d5! and White is helpless against ...b6 winning the errant knight.

14) 1 ♕h6+! ♗xh6 2 ♘h5 mate.

15) 1 ♕a4! as 1...♕xa4 2 ♘xe7 is mate and, meanwhile, Black is unable to cope with the threat to his queen. Full marks also for 1 ♕d4, 1 ♕e3 and 1 ♕f2, all with the same idea.

16) 1 ♕xe5! dxe5 2 ♖xd8+ mating.

17) 1 ♘f5! ♕xh5 2 ♘e7+ and 3 ♖xh5 mate.

18) 1 ♖h8+! ♔xh8 2 ♕h6+ ♔g8 3 ♕xg7 mate.

19) 1...♕xh3+! 2 ♔xh3 ♖h4+ 3 ♔g2 ♖h2 mate.

20) 1...♖a8 traps the white queen. White's only defence is 2 e5 when 2...♕xf3+ 3 ♔xf3 ♖xe8 leaves Black a piece ahead with an easy win.

21) 1 ♖d7! leaves Black with no good reply.

22) 1 ♘c5! and the black queen must abandon the defence of the bishop on c8.

23) 1 ♕d7+! ♗xd7 2 ♘xf7 mate.

24) 1 ♕c6! ♖b7 2 ♕e8+ ♔c7 3 ♕xe7+ and White quickly mates.

25) 1 g6+ hxg6 2 fxg6+ ♔f8 3 ♖e8 checkmate.

26) 1 ♗xg6+ fxg6 2 ♕e7+ ♔g8 3 ♖f8 checkmate.

27) 1...♕g2+! 2 ♖xg2 ♖e1+ mating.

28) 1...♖xg2! 2 ♖xg2 (otherwise 2...f2 will be crushing) 2...f2! and the pawn queens.

29) 1 ♖g7+! ♔xg7 (1...♘xg7 is met the same way) 2 ♕f8 mate.

30) 1...♕xh2+! 2 ♗xh2 ♖xg2+ 3 ♔h1 ♖gxh2+ 4 ♔g1 ♖g2 mate.

31) 1 ♕g5+! ♕g6 (1...♔f8 or 1...♔h8 2 ♕g8 is mate) 2 ♕xe7+ wins rook and bishop.

32) 1...♕xb3! 2 axb3 ♖a6+ mating.

33) 1 ♘b6+! axb6 2 ♕a6 checkmate.

34) 1 ♕g5+ ♕d5 2 ♖f5 wins the black queen.

35) 1 ♕xf8+! ♕xf8 2 ♖xh7 mate.

36) 1...♕g1+! 2 ♔h3 ♕df1+ 3 ♕g2 ♕h1 mate.

37) No! 1...♘xc3 walks into 2 ♗h7 checkmate.

38) Black wins with 1...♖xh3+ 2 gxh3 ♕xh3 mate.

39) 1...♛xh2+! 2 ♖xh2 ♖g1 mate.

40) 1 ♗f5! ♛xf5 2 ♛c7 mate.

Chapter Two

Moving On - Up to 1,200
Try to answer all the puzzles. Award yourself 30 Elo points for
each correct answer and a bonus of 5 Elo points if you solve the
puzzle in less than three minutes. If you score 1200 points (e.g. you
correctly solve all the positions without gaining any time bonuses),
you can clearly be confident that you are of experienced social
player standard. If you score less than 1200, review the answers
which caused you difficulty carefully before proceeding on the next
test.

I strongly suggest that you write down your solution to all positions on a separate sheet of paper and check them out once you
have completed the chapter. Otherwise the danger exists that you
will inadvertently spot solutions to later positions when checking
out the answers. Alternatively, if you wish to discover the answer to
each position immediately after you have solved it, I recommend
you use a sheet of paper to cover subsequent answers on the page
while checking the solution. The answers to chapter two start on
page 38.

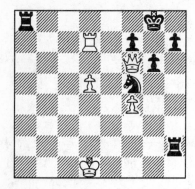

41) Black to play
Suetin - Hodgson, Hastings Premier 1991.
Here the white king is dangerously pinned down on the back rank. Can you see how Black forced a decisive material gain?

43) Black to play
Bogolyubov - Monticelli, San Remo 1930.
Despite having a rook less, Black forced a quick checkmate. What was his key first move?

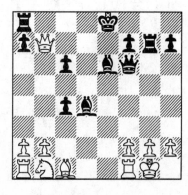

42) White to play
Nunn - Chandler, London 1985.
It appears that it is Black's king that should give him the greatest cause for concern. However, it is another feature of Black's position that causes his downfall. How did White continue?

44) Black to play
Shumov - Jaenisch, St Petersburg, 1849.
Black has a powerful concentration of forces on the kingside and finds a winning combination. Can you spot it?

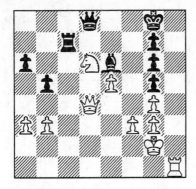

45) White to play
Meijers - Golubovic, Bern
1995.
In this spectacular position with
five pawns on the g-file, the
weak point is that Black's
queen is undefended. How can
White use this to his advantage?

47) White to play
Lautier - Sokolov, Linares
1995.
Here White found a neat combination which opened up the
black kingside defences and
allowed him to deliver a quick
checkmate. What did he play?

46) White to play
Dervishi - Cruceli, Berne 1995.
White has placed his pieces in
an aggressive posture on the
kingside and now cashed in
with a neat combination. Can
you see what he played?

48) Black to play
Tisdall - Gulko, San Francisco
1995.
The white king is horribly exposed to the attacking Black
forces. How did Black now
force victory with a clever tactical sequence?

49) Black to play
Chekhover - Lutikov, USSR 1951.
The key to this position is the unprotected state of the white queen on a6. How did Black exploit this?

51) White to play
Cvitan - Bischoff, Groningen 1980.
Here the black king has no moves available and White has a powerful pin on the a1-h8 diagonal. It is not surprising that White has an immediate win.

50) White to play
Quinteros - Tukmakov, Leningrad 1973.
How did White now obtain a decisive material advantage?

52) Black to play
Dorfman - Romanishin, USSR 1977.
How does Black, to play, break through the weakened White defences on the kingside?

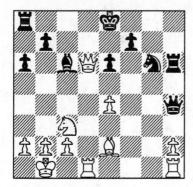

53) White to play
Brodsky - Nevednichy, Bucharest 1995.
Not all tactical continuations result in checkmate or the winning of pieces. Sometimes a tactic can be used to win just a pawn. This is one such case.

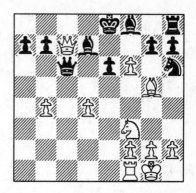

55) White to play
Duncan - Whiteley, St Peters de Beauvoir 1995.
White is a piece down but soon gained a decisive material advantage. Can you see how he achieved this?

54) White to play
Nunn - Georgiev, Linares 1988.
Black has just captured a piece but by doing so has fallen into his opponent's trap. How did White now make a decisive material gain?

56) Black to play
Steinitz - Rosenthal, London 1883.
Black has sacrificed a piece to tear away the protection from around the white king. How did he now capitalise?

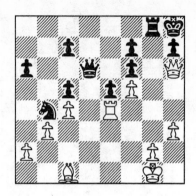

57) White to play
This is a variation is from Duras - Olland, Karlsbad 1907.
A discovered check can be a powerful weapon as it creates the possibility to move a piece to a square where, temporarily at least, it will be invulnerable.

59) White to play
Nunn - Portisch, Reykjavik 1988.
Although the black king is boxed in, it appears to be well defended. Can you spot how White broke through with a brilliant mating manoeuvre?

58) White to play
Chernin - Milov, Biel 1994.
White has steadily mounted an invasion of the weak points in the black camp and now finished off with a neat combination which won material. Can you spot it?

60) White to play
Alterman - Matlak, Moscow Olympiad 1995.
The pawn on d7 cuts off the Black pieces from the defence of his king. However, Black is threatening to capture it. Can you see how White struck first?

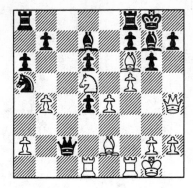

61) White to play
Gallagher - Schweizer, Bad Zurzach 1995.
England's Joe Gallagher has a reputation as a dangerous attacking player on the international circuit. How did he finish Black off here?

63) Black to play
Howell - Luther, Hastings 1995. Black has a powerful passed pawn on e3. How did he make the most of it?

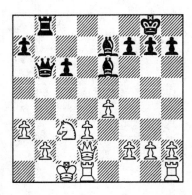

62) Black to play
Shamaev - Ufimtsev, Leningrad 1949.
It is often dangerous to have only one piece defending a key point, as that piece may be lured away by the opponent. This is the crux of this position.

64) White to play
Ornstein - Stean, Malmö 1979. Black has adopted a plan of sniping at the white centre from the wings - a dangerous strategy as it leaves his king vulnerable. How did White exploit this feature of the position?

65) Black to play
Foukakis - Moor, European
U-18 1994.
Black has sacrificed a piece to
lure the white queen away from
the defence of the king. What is
now the best way for Black to
continue?

67) White to play
Karpov - Salov, Linares 1993.
Here the FIDE World Cham-
pion Anatoly Karpov spotted a
clever way to capitalise on his
powerful kingside pressure.
What did he play?

66) Black to play
This is a variation from Pentium
Genius - Anand, Intel Grand
Prix, London 1994.
The Genius's extraordinary cal-
culating ability would not have
helped it here, as Black has a
quick kill. Can you see it?

68) Black to play
Steinsapir - Estrin, Moscow
1949.
Although Black is a piece
down, he has powerful play for
his pieces on the open lines on
the kingside. How did he now
make the most of his chances?

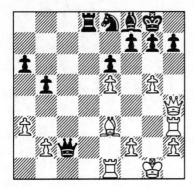

69) White to play
Polugaevsky - Antoshin, USSR 1955.
Here White spotted a weakness in the black position which gave him the chance for a winning combination. Can you do as well?

71) White to play
Borocz - Horvath, Budapest 1995.
Black has just carelessly captured a piece on f4 and thus fallen for a trap. How did White now close the net around the black king?

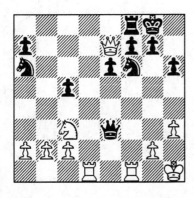

70) White to play
Lesiège - Norwood, Bermuda 1995.
How did White make the most of his open lines and the generally unco-ordinated state of the black pieces?

72) White to play
Marriott - Arnold, USA 1945.
White has launched an early attack but Black may have thought he had survived the worst. If so White's next would have swiftly disillusioned him.

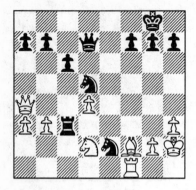

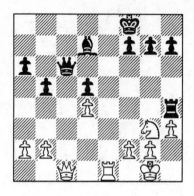

73) Black to play
Bondarevsky - Botvinnik, Leningrad 1941.
The black pieces have invaded some sensitive spots in the white position. How did Black now make the most of his active forces?

75) White to play
Botvinnik - Khavin, Moscow 1944.
The position looks quiet but, with a couple of accurate moves, White destroyed his opponent's defences. Can you see what he played?

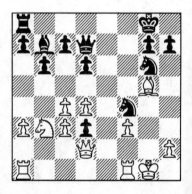

74) Black to play
Kotov - Botvinnik, Leningrad 1939.
Although Black is a pawn ahead, the opposite-coloured bishops seem to indicate a long struggle. However, Black's next move terminated the game.

76) Black to play
Branz - Goldenov, Minsk 1956.
The white kingside is exposed and this gave Black the chance for a winning combination. What was the key first move?

77) White to play
Keene - Martin, Simultaneous, Chelsea Arts Club 1995.
In this position, against Barry Martin, the captain of the Chelsea Arts Club chess team, from a recent simultaneous display, I forced a quick win. How?

79) White to play
Kennedy - Staunton, Brighton 1844.
How did White power his way through on the kingside to score a quick win?

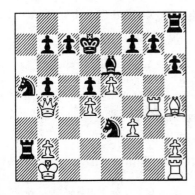

78) Black to play
Blake - Locock, Brighton 1884.
In this messy position, Black found a neat way to regain his queen. What did he play?

80) Black to play
Naumov - Petrushansky, USSR 1978.
Black has a dangerous attack against the white king. How did he make the most of his chances?

Solutions

41) 1...♖a1+! 2 ♕xa1 ♖h1+ wins.

42) 1 ♖h1! ♕g5 2 ♖h5 traps the black queen.

43) 1...♖f1+! 2 ♔xf1 ♕h1+ 3 ♔f2 ♘g4 mate.

44) 1...♖xg2+! 2 ♔xg2 ♕g6+ 3 ♔h1 (3 ♔f3 ♕g4 mate) 3...♗d5+ 4 f3 ♗xf3+! 5 ♖xf3 ♕g1 mate.

45) 1 ♖h8+! ♔xh8 2 ♘f7+ ♖xf7 3 ♕xd8+ and White wins easily on material.

46) 1 ♘xg6 hxg6 2 ♕xe6+! fxe6 3 ♗xg6 mate.

47) 1 ♘f5! gxf5 2 ♕g5+ ♔f8 3 ♖h6 and ♖h8 will inevitably follow.

48) 1...♘xe3+! 2 ♗xe3 ♕f3+ 3 ♗f2 ♖a2! and White loses, as 4 ♖c2 is met decisively by 4...♕d1+.

49) 1...♖xh2+! 2 ♔xh2 ♕h6+ 3 ♔g1 ♗xd4+ and the white queen is lost.

50) 1 ♖xd6+! wins, as if 1...cxd6 2 ♗g5+ ♔e6 3 ♖e7 is mate.

51) 1 ♕f7! and if 1...♖xf7 2 ♘xf7+ and 3 ♘xd8 wins for White. Meanwhile, Black has no defence against the threats of ♗xg7 mate, ♕xg7 mate or even ♕g8+.

52) 1...♗xf3+! 2 ♗xf3 ♗e5 with mate to follow on h2.

53) 1 ♗xa6! and if 1...♖xa6 2 ♕b8+ mates, while 1...bxa6 2 ♕xc6+ is hopeless. Black tried 1...♖d8 but after 2 ♕c5 ♖xd1+ 3 ♖xd1 White won easily with his two extra pawns.

54) 1 ♕h5+ ♔d8 2 ♗a5! and Black's queen is lost.

55) 1 ♕d8+! ♔xd8 (1...♔f7 2 ♘e5+) 2 fxg7+ ♔e8 3 gxh8♕ with a winning rook for bishop material advantage.

56) 1...♖xg3+! 2 hxg3 f2+ 3 ♔xf2 (3 ♕xf2 ♕h1 mate) 3...♕g2+ 4 ♔e3 ♕f3 mate.

57) 1 ♗f8+! ♗h5 2 ♕xh5+ gxh5 3 ♖h6 mate.

58) 1 ♘e7+! ♕xe7 2 ♖xc8 with an easy win.

59) 1 ♕xh7+! ♔xh7 2 ♖h4+ ♔g7 3 ♗h6+ ♔h7 4 ♗f8 mate.

60) 1 ♗xg7+! ♔xg7 2 ♕xh6+ and White quickly forces mate, e.g. 2...♔g8 3 ♖g6+ ♔f7 4 ♕g7.

61) 1 ♕h6! and if 1...♗xh6 2 ♘e7 is mate.

62) 1...♗g5! diverts the white queen from the defence of b2 and after 2 ♕xg5 ♕xb2 is mate. Note that 2 f4 ♗xf4! does not help the white cause.

63) 1...♖xd3! 2 ♖xd3 e2 and wins.

64) 1 ♘g6+! hxg6 2 ♖a3 and Black has no good counter against ♖h3+.

65) 1...♖e2! and if 2 ♗xe2 ♕g2 is mate. Otherwise, 2...♖g2+ will be decisive. Less accurate is 1...♕xd1 when 2 ♕xc5 allows White to struggle on.

66) 1...♖b1+ 2 ♔c2 ♖b2+! 3 ♔xb2 ♕xd2+ and Black wins.

67) 1 ♕xg6! hxg6 2 ♖h4 and ♖h8 mate is unstoppable.

68) 1...♕d2+! 2 ♗xd2 ♖f2+ mating.

69) 1 g6! ♕xg6+ 2 ♖g3 ♕d3 (Black must defend the loose rook on d8, but by doing so has walked into a deadly discovered attack) 3 ♗g5 and the rook goes.

70) 1 ♖xf6! gxf6 2 ♖d3 and the threat of the rook coming to the g-file is decisive, e.g. 2...♕e5 temporarily prevents ♖g3, but now 3 ♘e4! ♕xe4 4 ♖g3+ and wins.

71) 1 ♖xe8+ ♗xe8 2 ♖xe8+! ♕xe8 3 ♕d5+ ♕f7 4 ♕xa8+ and

White mates. Black's best chance is to give up his queen with 1 ♕xe8, when he will lose, but more slowly.

72) 1 ♕h6+! ♘xh6 2 ♗xh6+ ♔g8 3 f7 mate.

73) 1 ... ♖xh3+! (2 gxh3 ♘df4 and ... ♕xh3 mate).

74) 1...♕xg2+! 2 ♕xg2 ♖xe2 3 ♕xc6 bxc6 with an overwhelming material advantage.

75) 1 ♕g5! threatens the rook and ♕e7+. The only counter is 1...♕f6 but then 2 ♕xd5! leaves Black helpless against the threats of ♕xd7, ♕c5+ and ♕a8+.

76) 1...♕g4+! 2 ♔f2 (2 fxg4 ♘h3 mate) 2...♕xf3+ with a quick mate to follow.

77) 1 ♖xd5! and if 1...exd5 2 ♕xd5 is mate. At first sight 1 ♗b5 looks crushing, but Black defends with 1...♘e7.

78) 1...♖a1+! 2 ♔xa1 ♘c2+ 3 ♔b1 ♘xb4 with a material advantage.

79) 1 ♗xg6! hxg6 2 ♕xg6+ ♔h8 3 ♘h5 and Black is helpless as 3...♖g8 allows 4 ♕h6 mate.

80) 1...♗e4! 2 ♖f2 (if 2 ♕e7 f2+ 3 ♕xe4 f1♕! wins) 2...♖xa2! 3 ♖xa2 f2+ with a quick mate.

Chapter Three

Entering Competition - Up to 1,400

Try to answer all the puzzles. Award yourself 35 Elo points for each correct answer and a bonus of 5 Elo points if you solve the puzzle in less than three minutes. If you score 1400 points (e.g. you correctly solve all the positions without gaining any time bonuses), you can clearly be confident that you have the ability to challenge your home computer. If you score less than 1400, review the answers which caused you difficulty carefully before proceeding on the next test.

I strongly suggest that you write down your solution to all positions on a separate sheet of paper and check them out once you have completed the chapter. Otherwise the danger exists that you will inadvertently spot solutions to later positions when checking out the answers. Alternatively, if you wish to discover the answer to each position immediately after you have solved it, I recommend you use a sheet of paper to cover subsequent answers on the page while checking the solution. The answers to chapter three start on page 52.

81) Black to play
Horwitz - Staunton, London 1846.
Should Black play 1...fxg4 or does he have something stronger?

83) White to play
Nunn - Short, Brussels 1986. John Nunn has a fantastic score against Nigel Short. He has beaten Short on many occasions and never lost in a tournament game. How did he finish off the British number one here?

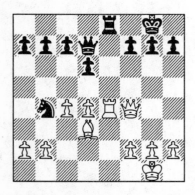

82) White to play
Nunn - Plaskett, London 1986. In this innocuous looking position, White found a neat move which won the game instantly. Can you see what he played?

84) White to play
Nunn - Portisch, Brussels 1986. Here White has to avoid a trap. He has two possible moves to win material: 1 ♖fe1 and 1 ♖de1, only one of which works. Which one, and why?

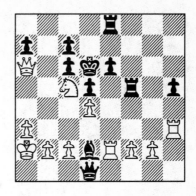

85) Black to play
Ljubojevic - Nunn, Szirak 1987.
Although Black has queen for rook and bishop, White's position is solid. Nevertheless, Black has a way to power through on the kingside. Can you find it?

87) White to play
Gerstner - Machelett, Germany 1994.
The black king has been driven into the middle of the board, but is apparently still quite well protected. How did White show that this is not the case?

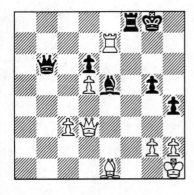

86) Black to play
Stefanova - Peptan, Moscow Olympiad 1995.
Things look desperate for Black, who is a pawn down and threatened with mate on h7. How did she turn the tables to score a neat win?

88) Black to play
Lepeshkin - Kosterin, Moscow 1961.
Black has already sacrificed a rook to tear open lines against the white king and now finishes off in fine style. Can you spot his brilliant next move?

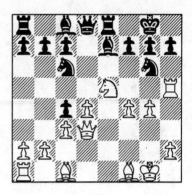

89) Black to play
Baburin - Adianto, Liechten-
stein 1993.
The open h-file provides the
key to this position. How did
Black, despite being a piece
down, force a quick checkmate?

91) White to play
Fox - Bauer, Washington 1901.
White is a piece down but has a
very aggressive posture on the
kingside. How did he now break
through in brilliant style?

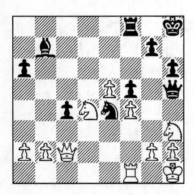

90) Black to play
Torres - Alekhine, Seville 1922.
How did Alekhine, Black to
play, finish the game with a
brilliant coup?

92) White to play
Mabbs - Alexander, London
1961.
White has tremendous threats
on the dark squares, particularly
along the a1-h8 diagonal. Can
you spot his winning combination?

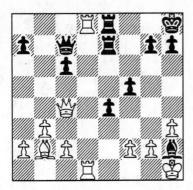

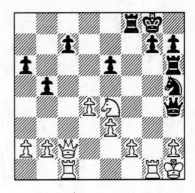

93) White to play
Szalanczy - Vanscura, Yugoslavia 1995
White's powerful bishop on b2 and Black's weak back rank are the decisive factors in this position. White to play and win.

95) Black to play
Schneizer - Cordes, Wiesbaden 1995.
Can you calculate the brilliant variation by which Black forced checkmate in five moves?

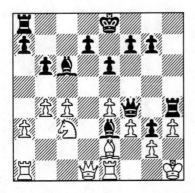

94) Black to play
Farago - Grooten, Hungary 1988.
How did Black break down the White fortress on the kingside with a series of powerful blows?

96) White to play
Almasi - Norwood, Germany 1994.
Combinations usually occur in positions with the queens on the board. Here White showed that one must also be on the lookout for tactics in the endgame.

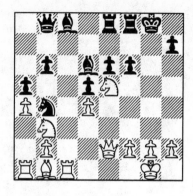

97) White to play
Puljek - Stanic, Porec 1994.
White has lured Black into a
trap by allowing a bishop move
to f6 which skewers his queen
and bishop. How did White now
demonstrate his refutation?

99) White to play
Wall - Smith, Four Nations
Chess League 1995.
Here White tore into the weakened Black kingside with a
powerful sacrifice. Can you see
how?

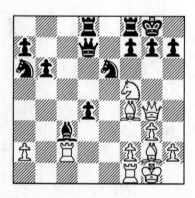

98) White to play
Szabolsci - Henttinen, Hungary
1981.
White has an impressive build-
up on the kingside but his winning blow came from another
direction. What did he play?

100) White to play
Dunworth - Summerscale, Four
Nations Rapid Play 1995.
Although queens have been exchanged, White has a very
strong attack against the black
king. What is his best continuation?

101) White to play
Smolnikov - Mitin, USSR 1977.
White's pieces are aimed dangerously at the black king. How did he capitalise on this to force a quick checkmate?

103) White to play
Richards - Lokok, Denmark 1975.
Can you spot White's clever tactical sequence which exploited the line-up of pieces along the a2-g8 diagonal?

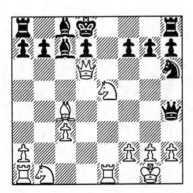

102) White to play
Schiffers - Jurewitsch, St Petersburg 1892.
White would like to play 1 ♘xf7 checkmate, but the black knight on h6 prevents this possibility. How did White overcome this problem?

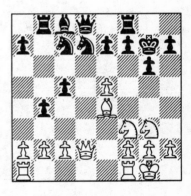

104) White to play
Carlier - Bernard, Brussels 1995.
Black has gone to sleep on the queenside so it is not surprising that White can now land a quick blow on the other wing. How did he continue?

105) Black to play
Schmidt - Helms, Germany
1925.
Although Black has powerful
play against the white king, es-
pecially on the long diagonal,
he is a rook down and must act
quickly. What is his best move?

107) White to play
Radulov - Soderborg, Helsinki
1961.
White's bishops, queen and
rook are all pointing menac-
ingly at the black kingside. How
did he make the most of this
concentration of force?

106) Black to play
Cochrane - Staunton, London
1842.
White must have been counting
on 1...♘xe6 2 ♕xd5 when
Black's pieces are suddenly
very exposed. However, Black
had a shock in store for him.

108) Black to play
Ashley - Korchnoi, San Francisco 1995.
Viktor Korchnoi, at age 63, is
the strongest active player aged
over 50 in the world. How did
he demonstrate his sharp tactical eye to force victory here?

109) White to play
This is a variation from Lasker - Steinitz, World Championship 1896.
White's immensely strong passed pawn on h7 gives him a winning position. Can you spot the cleanest kill?

111) White to play
A variation from Short - Kasparov, *Times* World Championship, London, game 8 1993.
Short generated a fantastic attack in this game, the key being the following position. What is White's winning continuation?

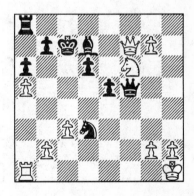

110) White to play
Alekhine - Bogolyubov, World Championship 1929.
White's pieces are converging on the black king. How did he land the killer blow?

112) White to play
This is a variation from Anand - Kasparov, Intel World Championship, game 3 1995.
Here White would like to promote with 1 g8=♕, but 1...♖xg8 2 ♕xg8 ♕xf6 is okay for Black. How can White improve?

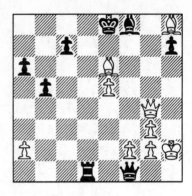

113) White to play
This is a variation from Kasparov - Anand, Intel World Championship, Game 10 1995. Black's king is very exposed, but if White does not act fast, he may find safety on the kingside. How can White avoid this?

115) White to play
This is again a variation from Kasparov - Anand, Intel World Championship, Game 10 1995. White is threatened with mate but it is his turn to move. How can he deliver a checkmate first?

114) White to play
This is another variation from Kasparov - Anand, Intel World Championship, Game 10 1995. How can White make decisive material gains by exploiting the unco-ordinated nature of the black forces?

116) White to play
Tarrasch - Von Gottschall, Dresden 1892.
The danger sign for Black in this position is that his king is completely boxed in and has no flight squares. How did White now continue?

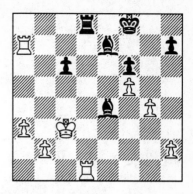

117) White to play
Mrdja - Luciani, San Giorgio
1995.
This position shows a typical
trick which Black must keep an
eye out for when he has castled
queenside. How did White
make a decisive breakthrough?

119) White to play
Speelman - Sax, Hastings Premier 1990.
Here White has obtained a very
promising endgame and now
forced an immediate win. Can
you see how?

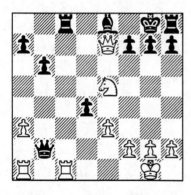

118) White to play
Geir - Olafsson, Reykjavik
1953.
White clearly has good tactical
chances, but must act quickly as
Black has threats himself. What
is White's strongest continuation?

120) White to play
Gallagher - Lane, Hastings
Masters 1990.
Joe Gallagher scored a grandmaster result in this tournament
on his way to eventually
claiming the title. How did he
force immediate victory here?

Solutions

81) 1...♖e2+! 2 ♗xe2 ♕xe2+ and ...♕xh2 mate.

82) 1 ♕f5! wins, e.g. 1...♖e6 (1...♕d8 2 ♖e7! forces mate) 2 d5 ♘xd3 3 dxe6 and White wins easily on material.

83) 1 ♖xg7+! ♔xg7 2 ♗h6+! and White forces mate either by 2...♔xh6 3 ♕h4+ ♔g7 4 ♕h7, or 2...♔g8 3 ♕xf8+ ♖xf8 4 ♖xf8.

84) 1 ♖de1? fails to 1...♖e8! 2 ♖xe4 ♗xg3+! 3 ♔xg3 ♖xe4. The correct path for White is 1 ♖fe1! and if Black tries the same trick with 1...♖e8 2 ♖xe4 ♗xg3+ 3 ♔xg3 ♖xe4 he gets mated after 4 ♖d8+.

85) 1...fxg3! tears the white king open with decisive consequences, as if 2 fxg4 ♖f2+ 3 ♔h3 ♖xh2 is mate.

86) 1...♕b1! 2 ♕e2 (2 ♕xb1 ♖f1 is mate) 2...♕e4 and White has no good move. 2...♕d1 also does the trick.

87) 1 ♕c8! leaves Black without a good reply as 1...♖xc8 allows 2 ♖xe6 checkmate.

88) 1...♕g5! wins, e.g. 2 ♘xg5 (2 ♖g1 ♕xg1+! 3 ♘xg1 ♘xf2 is mate) 2...♘xf2+ 3 ♔g1 ♘h3 mate.

89) 1...♖h1+! 2 ♔xh1 ♖h8+ 3 ♔g1 ♖h1+! 4 ♔xh1 ♕h8+ 5 ♔g1 ♕h2 checkmate.

90) 1...♕xh3! 2 gxh3 ♘f2+ 3 ♔g1 ♘xh3 mate.

91) 1 ♕xg6! hxg6 (1...fxg6 leads to a very similar finish, e.g. 2 ♗xc4+ ♔f8 3 ♘xg6+ hxg6 4 ♖h8 mate) 2 ♘xg6 fxg6 3 ♗xc4+ ♔f8 4 ♖h8 mate.

92) 1 ♗g7+! ♔xg7 2 ♘e8+ ♔h6 (2...♔g8 3 ♕g7 is mate) 3 ♕f4+ g5 4 ♕f6+ ♔h5 5 ♘g7+ ♔h4 6 ♕f2 mate.

93) 1 ♕f7! leaves Black without a sensible reply.

94) 1...♖xh3+! 2 gxh3 g2+ 3 ♔xg2 ♕g5+ and White gets mated,

e.g. 4 ♔h2 ♗f4+ 5 ♔h1 ♕g3 or 4 ♔h1 ♕g3 5 ♗f1 ♕g1.

95) 1...♕xh2+! 2 ♔xh2 ♘f4+ 3 ♔g3 ♖h3+ 4 ♔g4 h5+ 5 ♔g5 ♖f5 mate.

96) 1 ♘xf7+! and if 1...♔xf7 2 ♗h5 is checkmate.

97) 1 ♘h6+! ♔h8 (if 1...gxh6 2 ♕xf6 d4 3 ♖xd4 and White wins easily) 2 ♕xf6! gxf6 3 ♗xf6 mate.

98) 1 ♗c6! leaves the black queen helpless against an impending fork. Black tried 1...h5 but 2 ♕d1 left him with the same problem, e.g. 2...♕xc6 3 ♘e7+.

99) 1 ♗xh7+! ♔xh7 (declining the sacrifice doesn't help, e.g. 1...♔g7 2 ♕g4+ or 1...♔h8 2 ♕h5) 2 ♕h5+ ♔g8 3 ♕g6+ ♔h8 4 ♖c3 and mate is imminent.

100) 1 ♖xe5! is crushing, e.g. 1...♘xe5 (1...♗xd1 2 ♖d5+ ♘e5 3 ♗xe5+ ♔c6 4 ♖xd1+ is decisive) 2 ♗xe5+ ♔c8 3 ♘b6 checkmate.

101) 1 ♖xc6+! bxc6 2 ♗a6+! ♕xa6 3 ♕c7 mate.

102) 1 ♕xh6! ♕xc4 (of course not 1...gxh6 2 ♘xf7 mate) 2 ♕h4+! ♕xh4 3 ♘xf7 checkmate.

103) 1 ♘d8! ♖xd8 (1...♕xd5 2 ♖e8 is mate) 2 ♕xd8+ ♕f8 3 ♕d5+ ♕f7 4 ♖e8 mate.

104) 1 ♘h5+! gxh5 (1...♔h8 2 ♕h6 wins quickly) 2 ♕g5+ ♔h8 3 ♕xh5 f5 4 ♘g5 and mate is imminent.

105) 1...♕g2+! 2 ♔xg2 ♖xg3 mate.

106) 1...♘xh3+! 2 gxh3 ♖g4+! and mate follows.

107) 1 ♖xg7! ♔xg7 2 ♕g4+ ♔h8 3 ♗xf6+ ♗xf6 4 ♕h5 (or 4 ♕e4) and mate is inevitable.

108) 1...♘xb3+! 2 axb3 (2 ♕xb3 ♖xd4) 2...♖c5 and White is defenceless against an impending check on the a-file.

109) 1 ♖g4! ♖xh7 (if 1...♗b3 2 ♘f6) 2 ♖g8+ ♔d7 3 ♘f6+ and the rook goes.

110) 1 ♘e5+! ♘xe5 2 ♖a7+ and Black falls apart, as 2...♔c6 3 ♕e4 is mate.

111) 1 ♖xe6+! fxe6 2 ♕xe6+ and mate next move. 1...♗e7 2 ♖xe7+ is also disastrous.

112) 1 ♘d5+! wins for White, e.g. 1...♔c6 2 ♘e7+ picking up the queen or 1...♔b8 2 g8/♕+ with an easy win.

113) 1 ♗b2! wins immediately, as if 1...♕xb2 2 ♕xe6 is mate.

114) 1 ♗g5! wins at once. Full marks also for 1 ♗a3!.

115) 1 ♕h5+ ♔d8 2 ♗f6+ ♗e7 3 ♗xe7+ ♔xe7 4 ♕f7+ ♔d8 5 ♕f8 mate.

116) 1 ♕xh7+! (1 ♘xf7+! works equally well) 1...♘xh7 2 ♘xf7+ ♘xf7 3 ♘g6 mate.

117) 1 ♕xa6! destroys Black, as if 1...bxa6 2 ♗xa6+ regains the queen with a huge advantage.

118) 1 ♕xf7+! ♗xf7 2 ♖xc8+ mating.

119) 1 ♖xe7! ♔xe7 (1...♖xd1 2 ♖xe4) 2 ♖e1 and White emerges two pawns ahead with an easy win.

120) 1 ♘d7+ ♔a8 2 ♖c5! ♖xd7 (or 3 ♖a5 will be mate) 3 ♖c8 mate.

Chapter Four

Joining a Club - Up to 1,600

Try to answer all the puzzles. Award yourself 40 Elo points for each correct answer and a bonus of 5 Elo points if you solve the puzzle in less than three minutes. If you score 1600 points (e.g. you correctly solve all the positions without gaining any time bonuses), you can clearly be confident that you are of club player standard. If you score less than 1600, review the answers which caused you difficulty carefully before proceeding on the next test.

I strongly suggest that you write down your solution to all positions on a separate sheet of paper and check them out once you have completed the chapter. Otherwise the danger exists that you will inadvertently spot solutions to later positions when checking out the answers. Alternatively, if you wish to discover the answer to each position immediately after you have solved it, I recommend you use a sheet of paper to cover subsequent answers on the page while checking the solution. The answers to chapter four start on page 66.

121) Black to play
Evans - Staunton, London 1845.
Black to play concluded with a neat tactical sequence, despite the threat against his queen by the white knight. Can you work it out?

123) Black to play
This position is a variation from a game I played recently in a simultaneous display.
Black is hamstrung by the threat to his queen. How does he overcome this with a winning combination?

122) White to play
Staunton - Jaenisch, London 1851.
In this position, White used one of his pieces as a suicide bomber to prise open the black position. What did he play?

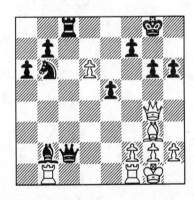

124) White to play
Engels - Maroczy, Dresden 1936.
How did White obtain a winning material advantage with a brilliant combination?

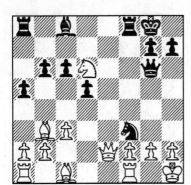

125) Black to play
Schonbauer - Despotovic, Yugoslavia 1974.
In this complicated position, Black is a piece down and both sides have a knight vulnerable to capture. What is Black's best move?

127) Black to play
Karic - Justin, USSR 1987.
Here Black won with a brilliant and unusual combination based on his pressure on the long diagonal. Can you see it?

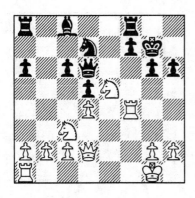

126) White to play
Gallagher - Koerant, Lyon 1993.
Not all combinations lead to checkmating attacks. Here White used a neat tactic to emerge with an easily winning endgame. What did he play?

128) White to play
Palatnik - Geller, USSR 1980.
Here White made use of the open g-file to deliver a surprisingly quick checkmate. Can you see how he continued?

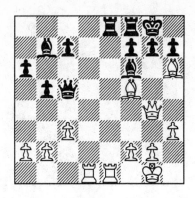

129) Black to play
Dorfman - Tseshkovsky, Tbilisi 1978.
In this complicated situation with both kings exposed Black has a neat combination to finish off the game. Can you see what he played?

131) White to play
Vasiukov - Cholmov, Moscow 1964.
The key here is the unprotected state of the black queen on c5. Can you see how White used this, combined with his kingside threats, to force a quick win?

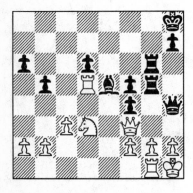

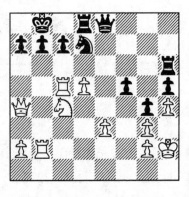

130) Black to play
S. Periera - R. Pereira, Portugal 1978.
Black has built up a very powerful concentration of force on the kingside and now broke through to score a quick win. Can you see how?

132) White to play
Khalifman - Serper, St. Petersburg 1994.
Here White bludgeoned his way through on the queenside with a series of sacrifices. Can you see how?

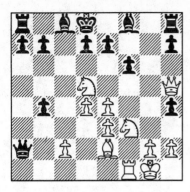

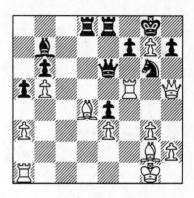

133) White to play
Buckley - Quillan, Four Nations
Chess League 1995.
Although Black is ahead on
material, he has only developed
his king and queen while the
white army is poised for attack.
How did White now cash in?

135) White to play
Botvinnik - Padevsky, Monte
Carlo 1968.
How did White capitalise on his
powerful passed pawn on g7?

134) White to play
Miles - Nedobora, Seville 1994.
White is a piece and two pawns
down and his knight on e4 is
pinned. Can he salvage any-
thing from this apparent disas-
ter?

136) White to play
This is a variation from Alekhine - Rubinstein, Karlsbad
1923.
White is a piece down. Should
he recapture on b4, or has he
got something better?

137) Black to play
Mayet - Kennedy, London
1851.
Here Black alertly spotted an
opportunity to win a key pawn.
What did he play?

139) White to play
Solin - Lasarev, Vienna 1994.
How did White force a quick
checkmate?

138) White to play
Keene - Kester George, Simul-
taneous display against twenty
opponents, Athenaeum 1995.
Can you spot they key move of
White's winning combination?
White's idea is based on the
weakness of the black back row.

140) White to play
Ninov - Berovsky, Bulgaria
1995.
In this position Black has sacrificed material for an attack so it
is surprising that it was actually
White who scored with a winning tactic. What did he play?

141) White to play
Pagantoniov - Routilin, Athens
1937.
In this position White concluded the game with a brilliant
combination which forced
checkmate. Can you see what
he played?

143) White to play
Nunn - Seirawan, Monaco
1994.
Black had assumed that White
would play 1 ♔e2 here, when
the exposed white king would
give him good chances. How
did White disillusion him?

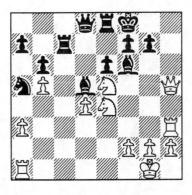

142) White to play
Kaidanov - Anand, Moscow
1987.
White has already sacrificed a
piece to weaken the black
king's defences. Can you see
how he now finished off with a
further sacrifice?

144) White to play
This is a variation from the
game Alekhine - Capablanca,
World Championship 1927.
Endgames with few pieces on
the board are not always devoid
of tactical possibilities. What is
White's most elegant win?

145) White to play
This is a variation from Short -
Kasparov, *Times* World Championship London 1993.
White seems to have lost his
queen as it is pinned against the
white king. What did Nigel
have planned for this position?

147) White to play
Alekhine - Bogolyubov, World
Championship 1934.
How did Garry Kasparov's
hero, the great world champion
Alekhine, break through in this
endgame?

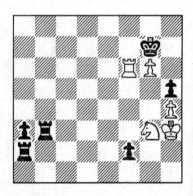

146) White to play
Alekhine - Bogolyubov, World
Championship 1929.
There is a well-known saying in
chess that the king is a strong
piece. How did White capitalise
on the active position of his
king here?

148) White to play
Bogolyubov - Alekhine, World
Championship 1934.
Black, with his two powerful
rooks and two passed pawns is
winning easily. As a last ditch
defence, White tried 1 ♖xf2.
Should Black capture this rook?

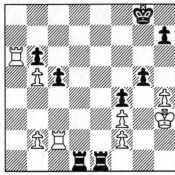

149) Black to play
Bogolyubov - Alekhine, World
Championship 1929.
The black rooks have got in
'round the back'. Can you spot
the key move that enabled
Black to close the net around
the white king?

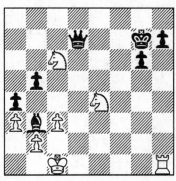

151) White to play
This is a variation from Short -
Kasparov, *Times* World
Championship, Game 10 1993.
It appears that White's attack
has burnt out, but he has a final,
winning trick up his sleeve. Can
you spot it?

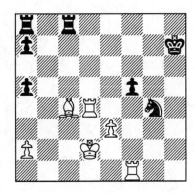

150) White to play
A variation from Kasparov -
Short, *Times* World Championship, London, game 9 1993.
One should always be on the
lookout for tactical opportuni-
ties, even in the endgame. This
position is a case in point.

152) Black to play
This is a variation from Short -
Kasparov, *Times* World
Championship, game 12, 1993.
Although Black has a passed
pawn on h2, the white one on c6
appears the more dangerous.
How can Black save the day?

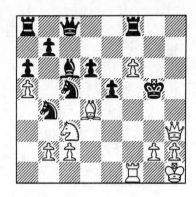

153) White to play
This is a variation from Kasparov - Short, *Times* World Championship, Game 15, 1993. Short had already resigned before this position could arise. What is the win that he didn't want to have shown to him?

155) White to play
This is another variation from Anand - Kasparov, Intel World Championship, game 3, 1995. White has sacrificed a rook and a piece to draw the black king into the open. How can he now force a quick mate?

154) White to play
This is a variation from Anand - Kasparov, Intel World Championship, game 3 1995. How could White now act swiftly before Black had a chance to co-ordinate his position?

156) Black to play
This is a variation from Anand - Kasparov, Intel World Championship, Game 13 1995. The white king is stuck in the centre and is threatened by the dangerous black rooks. How can Black exploit this?

157) Black to play
This is another variation from
Anand - Kasparov, Intel World
Championship, Game 13, 1995.
Anand had already resigned this
game without wishing to see the
conclusion that Kasparov had in
store for him here.

159) White to play
Bareev - Kosten, Hastings
Premier 1990.
White has a very active position
and now forced a decisive
breakthrough. Can you see what
he played?

158) White to play
Cheron - Polikier, Chamonix
1927.
The black king is stuck in the
centre, while White's forces are
fully co-ordinated and have
adopted threatening positions.
How did White now win?

160) White to play
Agdestein - Hodgson, Hastings
Premier 1991.
As well as being a top chess
player, Norweigan Simen Agdestein, has also played international football. Here he shows
his chess skill with a fine finish.

Solutions

121) 1...♘e1+! 2 ♘xc6 (2 ♔g1 ♕h1+ 3 ♔xh1 ♖f1+ 4 ♗g1 ♗f3+ 5 ♕g2 ♗xg2 mate) 2...♖f1+ 3 ♗g1 ♗f3+ 4 ♕g2 ♗xg2 mate.

122) 1 ♘e5! wins, e.g. 1...fxe5 2 ♕f6+ ♔e8 3 ♖xh8+ ♔e7 4 ♕f8 mate, or 1...dxe5 2 ♕xf6+ ♔d6 3 ♖fd1 again mating.

123) 1...♕h2+! 2 ♔xh2 ♖xf2+ 3 ♔h1 ♘g3+ 4 ♔g1 ♖ee2 and mate with...♖g2 follows.

124) 1 ♖xb2! ♕xb2 2 ♕xc8+! ♘xc8 3 d7 and the pawn queens.

125) 1...♗h3! wins, e.g. 2 gxh3 (2 ♗g5 ♗xg2+! 3 ♔xg2 ♕xg5+ 4 ♔h1 ♕h6 is decisive) 2...♕xd6 and the threat against h2 is also decisive.

126) 1 ♖xf7+! ♖xf7 2 ♖xh6+! ♔g8 (if 2...♔xh6 3 ♘xf7+ as in the main line) 3 ♕h8+! (White is insistent!) 3...♔xh8 4 ♘xf7+ ♔g7 5 ♘xd6 with two extra pawns and an easy win.

127) 1...♖xg2! 2 ♗xg2 ♕c6! and if 3 ♗xc6 ♗xc6 is mate. White tried 3 ♘f4, but after 3...exf4 4 ♕d2 f3 5 ♗xd4 fxg2+ he had a hopeless position.

128) 1 ♖xg7+! ♔xg7 2 ♕g4+ ♔h8 3 ♕f5 and ♕xh7 mate cannot be prevented.

129) 1...♔f2+! 2 ♕xb3 ♘g5+! 3 hxg5 ♕h8 mate. Also, full marks for 1...♘g5+ 2 hxg5 ♔f2+ 3 ♔h4 (3 ♕xb3 ♕h8 is mate) 3...♕h8 mate.

130) 1...♖g3! 2 fxg3 ♕xh2+! 3 ♔xh2 ♖h6+ 4 ♕h5 ♖xh5 mate.

131) 1 ♗xg7! ♗xg7 2 ♕h5 h6 3 ♗h7+ and the black queen goes.

132) 1 ♖xb7+! ♔xb7 2 ♖xc7+! ♔xc7 3 ♕xa7+ ♔c8 4 d6 and now 5 ♕c7 mate can only be prevented by 4...♖xd6 when 5 ♘xd6 is still mate.

133) 1 ♘e5! is decisive, as 1...fxe5 2 ♕xe5 ♖g8 3 ♖xf8+ leads to mate as does 1...d6 2 ♘f7+ ♔d7 3 ♗b5+ ♔e6 4 ♘f4.

134) 1 ♖f8+! ♖xf8 2 ♖xf8+ ♔xf8 3 ♕f7+! ♔xf7 leads to a draw by stalemate.

135) 1 ♕xh7+! ♔xh7 2 ♖h5+ ♔g8 3 ♖h8+ ♘xh8 4 gxh8♕ mate.

136) 1 ♕h4+ ♔g8 2 ♕h7+ ♔f8 3 ♕h8+ ♔e7 4 ♕xg7+ ♔e8 (4 ... ♔d6 5 ♖fd1+) 5 ♕g8+ ♗f8 6 ♕xg6+ mating.

137) 1...♘xe5! and if 2 ♗xb6 ♘f3+, when White cannot regain his pawn with 3 ♔f2 ♘xd2 4 ♗xa7 because of 4...g5, winning a piece.

138) 1 ♖a6! ♕xa6 (if 1...♕b1+ 2 ♔h2 ♖f8 3 ♖xf6! wins: or 1...♕b8 also 2 ♖xf6!) 2 ♖xd8+! ♗xd8 3 ♕f8 checkmate.

139) 1 ♖h8+! ♗xh8 2 ♕h1 ♖fd8 3 ♕h7+ and mate next move.

140) 1 ♕xc6+! bxc6 2 ♗a6+ ♔d7 3 ♖b7+ and White emerges a piece ahead.

141) 1 ♕e6! ♘xe6 2 ♘g6+ hxg6 3 ♖h3+ ♔g8 4 ♗xe6+ ♔f8 5 ♖h8 mate.

142) 1 ♕xf7+! ♖xf7 2 ♘g6+ ♔g8 3 ♖h8 mate.

143) 1 ♕xf3! gxf3 2 ♗b5+ ♔e7 (if 2...♕d7 White will win on material) 3 ♗g5 mate.

144) 1 ♖f5! ♖xf5 2 exf5 h2 3 f8♕ h1♕ 4 ♕a8+ and the black queen is skewered. 1 ♔e7 and 1 ♖h8 will also win, but more laboriously.

145) 1 ♕xc6! bxc6 2 ♖d8 mate.

146) 1 ♖d3+! ♔e7 2 ♔c7 and Black loses a piece.

147) 1 f6+! ♔e8 (1...♔d6 or 1...♔d8 are met by 2 f7) 2 ♗g6+ ♔d8 3 f7 and the pawn goes through.

148) No! 1...♖xf2 would lead to stalemate. Instead Alekhine played 1 ♖xf2 ♖xg3+ 2 ♔xg3 ♖xf2 3 ♔xf2 a2 and the pawn queens.

149) 1...h5! leaves White helpless against 2...♖h1+ and 3...♖dg1

mate.

150) 1 ♗e6! sets up dual threats against c8 and f5. Black can try 1...♖c2+ but this fails to 2 ♔d3 ♖f2 3 ♖xf2 ♘xf2+ 4 ♔e2 and, remarkably, the black knight is trapped.

151) 1 ♖xh7+! ♔xh7 2 ♘f6+ leaves White a piece ahead.

152) 1...♖c2! draws after 2 ♖xc2 h1♕ 3 c7 ♕e1+ and White cannot escape the checks.

153) 1 ♕f6+! wins the bishop on d5.

154) 1 ♕h4! creates dual threats of 2 ♕d8+ and 2 ♕xb4 and wins, e.g. 1...♘d5 2 ♘xd5 ♗xd5 3 ♕d8+ or 1...♖g7 2 ♕d8+ mating (and not 2 ♕xb4 ♖xg6 when Black has reasonable chances).

155) 1 ♗e3+! ♔g6 2 ♕h6+ ♔f7 3 ♕g7+ ♔e6 4 ♕e7 checkmate.

156) 1...♖xe2+! 2 ♖xe2 ♕g1 mate.

157) 1...♖xe4+ 2 ♗e2 ♕f2+ 3 ♔d1 ♖xe2 4 ♕xe2 ♖d6+ with an easy win on material.

158) 1 ♘c7+! ♘xc7 2 ♖xe7+ ♔xe7 3 ♕f6+ ♔e8 and now White has the choice of three mating moves: 4 ♗xf7, 4 ♖d8 and 4 ♕d8.

159) 1 ♘xd6! ♕xd6 2 ♖hd1 ♕e7 3 ♕e5+ is decisive.

160) 1 fxg5! ♖xg4 2 ♗f6 and mate is inevitable.

Chapter Five

Playing Matches - Up to 1,800
Try to answer all the puzzles. Award yourself 45 Elo points for each correct answer and a bonus of 5 Elo points if you solve the puzzle in less than three minutes. If you score 1800 points (e.g. you correctly solve all the positions without gaining any time bonuses), you can clearly be confident that you are a strong club player or able to represent your region. If you score less than 1800, review the answers which caused you difficulty carefully before proceeding on the next test.

I strongly suggest that you write down your solution to all positions on a separate sheet of paper and check them out once you have completed the chapter. Otherwise the danger exists that you will inadvertently spot solutions to later positions when checking out the answers. Alternatively, if you wish to discover the answer to each position immediately after you have solved it, I recommend you use a sheet of paper to cover subsequent answers on the page while checking the solution. The answers to chapter five start on page 80.

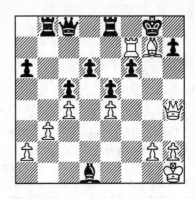

161) White to play
Staunton - Harrison, London 1840.
White has opened up lines against the black king but his rook and bishop are both attacked. How did he respond?

163) White to play
Tal - Rantanen, Tallinn 1979. Mikhail Tal was one of the great attacking geniuses and the chess world was much saddened by his death in 1992. This finish is typical. How did Tal deliver the killing blow?

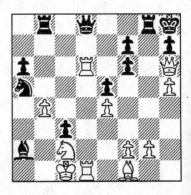

162) White to play
Nguyen - Züger, Moscow Olympiad 1995.
White has dangerous attacking chances along the open h-file. How did he now make use of these with a forcing combination?

164) White to play
Feher - Priehoda, Budapest 1994.
Brilliant play can sometimes been seen in defence rather than attack and here is such a case. White is threatened with ...♘b3 mate. What is his best move?

165) White to play
Parr - Wheatcroft, London
1938.
In this position White finished
the game with a beautiful, geo-
metric combination. What was
the decisive first move?

167) White to play
Lochmer - Karner, Leningrad
1940.
How did White use the open h-
file to bring his attack against
the black king to a decisive
conclusion?

166) White to play
Bronstein - Geller, USSR 1961.
How did White power his way
through in this seemingly cha-
otic situation?

168) White to play
This puzzle was composed by
Locock in Brighton 1896.
Although White has a crushing
material superiority, the point of
the problem is that he must give
checkmate in two moves. He
only has one way to do this.

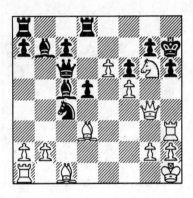

169) White to play
Taunton - Minchin, Brighton
1888.
Although the black king has
been driven into the open, the
white bishop on a2 is not par-
ticipating in the game. How did
White activate this piece?

171) White to play
Andrews - Bowley, Brighton
1889.
White has an aggressive position on the kingside and now
exploited this with a powerful
series of sacrifices. Can you see
how he continued?

170) Black to play
Downer - Pierce, Sussex
Championship 1884.
In this position, Black finished
off with a brilliant move, ex-
ploiting the weakness of
White's back rank. can you see
what he played?

172) White to play
Field - Raoux, Brighton 1914.
Although the game is barely out
of the opening the position, with
various pins and attacked
pieces, has already become very
complex. What is White's best
move?

173) White to play
Keene - Bond, Simultaneous display against twenty opponents, Athenaeum 1995.
How does White exploit the exposed situation of the black king to force a quick checkmate?

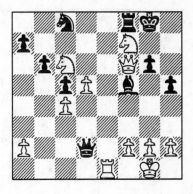

175) White to play
Van Hennig - Lucke, Hannover 1936.
White has a strong attack but his knight on f7 is pinned, his rook on e1 is under attack and his back rank is weak. How did he deal with these problems?

174) White to play
Gulko - Short, Novgorod 1995.
Here White resigned but several *Times* readers suggested that White could draw with 1 ♔b6 ♘d6 2 ♔c7 ♔e6 3 h6. What is the flaw in this plan?

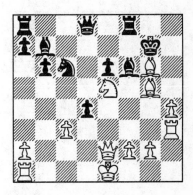

176) White to play
Alekhine - Koenig, Vienna 1922.
White has a winning attack, but what is the most direct way to end matters?

177) Black to play
Peterson - Skula, Riga 1950.
It looks as if Black must retreat his queen when White will be able to pursue his own plans by capturing on e6. Black, however, side-stepped this by spotting a clever combination.

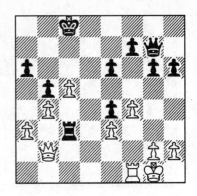

179) White to play
Alekhine - Capablanca, World Championship 1927.
White has caught the black rook in a nasty pin. What is the most efficient way to exploit this?

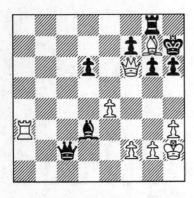

178) White to play
This is a variation from Anand - Kamsky, Las Palmas 1995.
White has made serious inroads into the black kingside. How can he now finish the game with an interesting tactical sequence?

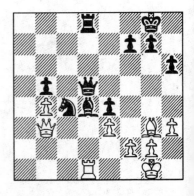

180) Black to play
Capablanca - Alekhine, World Championship 1927.
Black is a piece ahead, but it looks as if White is poised to regain it due to the pin along the d-file. However, Black found a way to escape with his booty.

181) Black to play
This is a variation from Short -
Kasparov, *Times* World
Championship, Game 12, 1993.
Can you spot the clever con-
tinuation that Black had in mind
here in order to pursue his
queenside initiative?

183) White to play
A variation from the game
Short - Kasparov, *Times* World
Championship, game 8, 1993.
If Short had been happy to draw
this game (which he was not) he
could have done so here with a
beautiful queen sacrifice. How?

182) Black to play
This is a variation from Short -
Kasparov, *Times* World
Championship, game 10, 1993.
Black can capture the white
rook on d1 with check but, ac-
tually, he has a much stronger
continuation. What is it?

184) Black to play
This is a variation from Short -
Kasparov, *Times* World
Championship, Game 14, 1993.
White has an extra piece but
this material is not helping to
defend his king. How can Black
exploit this?

185) White to play
This is a variation from Kasparov - Anand, Intel World Championship, game 8, 1995. In this complex endgame, White has good play thanks to his advanced pawns. How can he make the most of this?

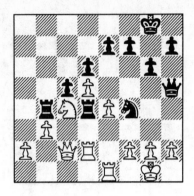

187) Black to play
Lovass - Titkos, Hungary 1971. How did Black make the most of his active pieces with a clever combination?

186) White to play
This is a variation from Kasparov - Anand, Intel World Championship, Game 10, 1995. White has a ferocious attack with his three pieces combining against the Black king. Can you spot a clear win for White?

188) Black to play
Hermann - Brun, East Germany 1974.
It looks as if Black might be in trouble as his king is horribly exposed and his pieces threatened. How did he turn the tables with a swift counter-attack?

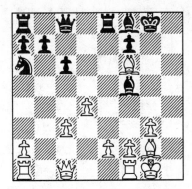

189) White to play
Chiburdanidze - Sharif, Lipp-
stadt 1995.
White has sacrificed a piece to
open up the black kingside. Can
you spot her key winning
move?

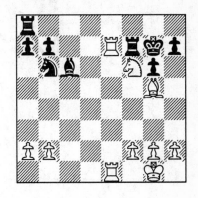

191) White to play
Martinovic - Schwing, St. Inge-
bert 1995.
Can you see how White made
the most of his active pieces in
this endgame?

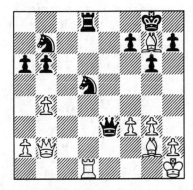

190) Black to play
Vilela - Spiridonov, Varna
1977.
White's back row is slightly
vulnerable. How did Black
cleverly use this possibility to
force a quick win?

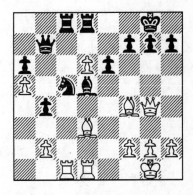

192) White to play
Tukmakov - Speelman, Tilburg
Blitz 1994.
The black kingside is danger-
ously unprotected. How did
White exploit this with a clever
combination?

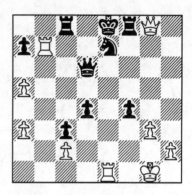

193) White to play
Chemelinsky - Kabiatansky,
USSR 1989.
This looks like an innocent
position, but White spotted a
clever winning continuation
based on the weakness of
Black's back row.

195) White to play
Hartston - Whiteley, England
1974.
In the early seventies, chess
journalist William Hartston was
known as a dangerous attacking
player. Here is an example of
his dynamic play.

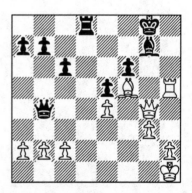

194) Black to play
Yanowsky - Toriran, Canada
1953.
Although White is two pawns
ahead his queenside pieces are
still asleep, so it is not surprising that he has a winning combination. Can you spot it?

196) White to play
Petrosian - Moldagaliev, USSR
1970.
Although ex-world champion
Tigran Petrosian was mainly
known as an outstanding
strategist, he was also a brilliant
tactician. Here is an example.

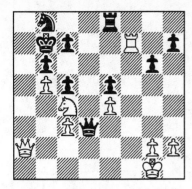

197) White to play
Shianovsky - Porgebinsky, Kiev
1955.
Can you see how White broke
into his opponent's position to
deliver a quick checkmate?

199) White to play
Chandler - Olafsson, Hastings
Premier 1990.
White has advanced his e-pawn
into the heart of the black position. He now found a tactical
sequence to exploit the strength
of this pawn and win quickly.

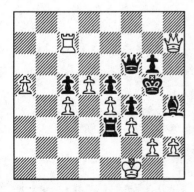

198) White to play
Plaskett - Velimirovic, Banja
Luka 1985.
White has sacrificed a piece to
drive the black king up the
board. How did he now finish
the game off with a checkmating combination?

200) White to play
Spraggett - Speelman, Hastings
Premier 1989.
Here White played 1 ♘xg3?,
overlooking the chance for a
brilliant finish. Can you see an a
move which would have deliv-
ered a brilliant coup de grace?

Solutions

161) 1 ♗d4! ♕xe2 2 ♖xf7+ ♔g8 3 ♖g7+ ♔h8 4 ♖g6+ mating swiftly.

162) 1 ♖h7+! ♔xh7 2 ♕h1+ ♔g8 3 ♕h6 (threatening ♕xg6+) 3...♘ce5 4 ♖h1. Now the threats on the h-file are unstoppable and Black could only give a few harmless checks: 4...♘xf3+ 5 ♔d1 ♘xb2+ 6 ♔c1 ♘d3+ 7 ♔b1 and White wins.

163) 1 ♗h8! ♔xf7 2 ♕xf6+ and 3 ♕g7 mate.

164) 1 ♗c4! throws a spanner in the works. If 1...♘xc4 or 1...♗xc4 White safely captures the black queen with 2 ♖xd8. If Black saves the queen with 1...♕e7 then 2 ♗xa2 wins a piece for White.

165) 1 ♖h5! threatens 2 ♖xh6+! and if 2 gxh5 ♕f5 is mate.

166) 1 ♕g6! fxg6 2 ♖xg7+ ♔f8 (2...♔h8 is met the same way) 3 ♘xg6 mate. Also give yourself full marks if you found the alternative solution 1 ♖xf7! meeting 1...♖xd3 with 2 ♖xg7+ and 3 ♘g6 as in the game, or 1...♔xf7 with 2 ♕g6+.

167) 1 ♖xh6+! ♔xh6 2 ♕f4+ g5 (2...♕g5 3 ♕h2+ wins the black queen) 3 ♕h2+ ♔g6 4 ♕h5+ ♔f6 5 ♕f7 mate.

168) 1 ♕b4 gives mate next move against any Black reply.

169) 1 ♖xb5! ♔xb5 2 ♖b1+ ♔a4 (otherwise 3 ♕b6+ will win) 3 ♗xc4! ♔a3 (if 3...dxc4 4 ♕xc4+ forces mate) 4 ♕b6.

170) 1...♕xa2! leaves White without a reasonable reply.

171) 1 ♗xh6! gxh6 2 ♘f8+! ♗xf8 3 ♕g6+ ♔h8 4 ♕xf6+ ♔h7 5 ♕f7+ ♔h8 6 ♖g3 and mate follows.

172) 1 ♘xe5! wins a piece by force, the main variation being 1...♗xd1 2 ♘xc6+ ♔f8 3 ♘xd8 ♖xd8 4 ♗d3 and Black, unable to defend both bishops, must lose one of them.

173) 1 ♘xe5+! dxe5 2 ♕c4+ ♔d7 (2...♔b7 3 ♕xa6 mate) 3 ♕d5+ ♔c8 4 ♗xa6+ ♖b7 5 ♕xb7+ ♔d7 6 ♕d5+ and mate follows.

174) After 1 ♔b6 ♘d6 2 ♔c7, Black simply continues with 2...b5! and although White can capture the black knight, the black b-pawn will promote.

175) 1 ♕h8+! ♔xf7 2 ♖e7+! ♘xe7 3 ♕h7+ ♔e8 4 ♕xe7 mate.

176) 1 ♗h6+! and the bishop cannot be captured on account of ♕h5+ and mate next move. Black played 1...♔g8 but after 2 ♘xc6 ♗xc6 3 ♕xe6+ ♔h8 4 ♗xf8 was a rook in arrears.

177) 1...♕xf3! 2 gxf3 exd5 and the combined threats of...♗h3 mate and...dxc4 will leave Black a piece to the good.

178) 1 ♗h8! ♗c4 (if 1...♖xh8 2 ♕xf7 mate and meanwhile, White threatens 2 ♕xf7+ ♔xh8 3 ♖a7) 2 ♖a8! and Black has no defence.

179) The immediate 1 ♖c1 fails because 1...♖xc1+ is check. 1 ♔f2!, however, leaves Black defenceless against the coming ♖c1, e.g. 1...♕f6 2 g3 and Black has no more tricks. Also give yourself full marks for 1 ♖f2 with the plan of ♖c2.

180) 1...♘xe3! wins, as if 2 ♕xd5 ♖xd5 3 fxe3 ♗xe3+ picks up the rook.

181) 1...♖xb4! and if 2 ♕xb4 f3+ wins the white queen.

182) 1...♕f4+! 2 ♖6d2 (2 ♔b1 ♕xd6 is terrible for White) 2...exd1♕+ 3 ♔xd1 ♕f1 mate.

183) 1 ♖xf7 ♕xe6 2 ♖g7+ ♔f8 3 ♖f7+ with a perpetual check draw.

184) 1...♕f5! 2 ♖f1 ♕c5+ 3 ♔h1 ♕e3 and mate follows swiftly.

185) 1 dxc7! ♖xc7 (if Black does not capture this pawn, e.g. 1...♖e8 then 2 ♗d6 leaves White with an overwhelming material and positional advantage) 2 ♗d6 ♖xc6+ 3 dxc6+ ♔xc6 4 ♗xe5 and White emerges a piece ahead.

186) 1 ♗c3! leaves Black without a defence, e.g. 1...g6 2 ♕f3+; 1...♖hg8 2 ♕f5+ or 1...♖h6 2 ♕f3+.

187) 1...♖bxc4! 2 bxc4 ♖xd2 3 ♕xd2 ♕g5 and the dual threats of...♕xg2 and...♘h3+ are decisive.

188) 1...♖h2+! 2 ♔xh2 (2 ♘xh2 ♕g2 mate) 2...♕xb2+ 3 ♔h1 ♕xc1+ 4 ♔g2 ♕g1+ 5 ♔f3 ♕f1+ winning.

189) 1 ♗h3! creates insoluble problems for Black as if 1...♗xh3 2 ♕g5+ forces mate.

190) 1...♘f6! sets White insoluble problems, e.g. 2 ♖xd8+ ♘xd8 and now the bishop on g7 is lost as 3 ♗xf6 ♕e1+ leads to mate.

191) 1 ♗h6+! ♔xf6 (otherwise Black loses his rook) 2 ♖1e6+ ♔f5 3 ♖e5+ ♔g4 4 h3+ ♔h4 5 ♗g5+ ♔h5 6 g4 mate.

192) 1 ♖xc5! ♖xc5 2 ♕h4 and White wins, e.g. 2...f6 3 ♕xh7+ ♔f8 4 ♕h8+ ♔f7 5 ♕xd8.

193) 1 ♘f5! exf5 (1...♘xf5 2 ♕xc8+) 2 ♕xc8+! ♘xc8 3 ♖e8 mate.

194) 1...♕xf2+! 2 ♖xf2 ♖e1+ 3 ♖f1 ♗h2+ 4 ♔h1 ♖xf1 mate.

195) 1 ♕g6! ♕xg6 2 ♖exe7+ ♔d8 3 ♖bd7 mate.

196) 1 ♖h8+! ♔xh8 2 ♕h5+ ♔g8 3 ♗e6+ ♔f8 4 ♕f7 mate.

197) 1 ♕a7+! ♔xa7 2 ♖xc7+ ♔a8 3 ♘xb6 mate.

198) 1 ♕xh4+! ♔xh4 2 ♖h7+ ♔g5 3 h4 mate.

199) 1 ♖d8! ♖xd8 2 ♖xc7! and White wins a piece, as 2...♕xc7 3 e8♕+ ♖xe8 4 ♕xe8 is mate.

200) 1 ♘g5! wins as if 1...♗xh2 2 ♖xh7+ ♕xh7 3 ♘xf7 is mate.

Chapter Six

International Standard - Towards 2,000

Try to answer all the puzzles. Award yourself 50 Elo points for each correct answer and a bonus of 5 Elo points if you solve the puzzle in less than five minutes. If you score 2000 points (e.g. you correctly solve all the positions without gaining any time bonuses), you can clearly be confident that you are of international rating standard and capable of achieving a published international rating.

I strongly suggest that you write down your solution to all positions on a separate sheet of paper and check them out once you have completed the chapter. Otherwise the danger exists that you will inadvertently spot solutions to later positions when checking out the answers. Alternatively, if you wish to discover the answer to each position immediately after you have solved it, I recommend you use a sheet of paper to cover subsequent answers on the page while checking the solution. The answers to chapter six start on page 94.

201) Black to play
Kennedy - Staunton, London 1845.
Black has sacrificed his queen to set up a powerful attack on the g1-a7 diagonal. Now his bishop on b6 is attacked. How did he deal with this?

203) White to play
Lushovsky - Griedner, USSR 1976.
White has chances based on the vulnerability of Black's back rank. Can you see what he played? Be careful - there is a trap in the position.

202) White to play
Nunn - Hansen, Næstved 1985.
Here Nunn won with a brilliant move, exploiting the strength of his major pieces on the g-file. This is a difficult problem, so congratulations if you spot White's ingenious win.

204) White to play
Spassky - Milic, Dresden 1964.
This is a tricky endgame position. If White plays 1 b8=♕ ♗xb8+ 2 ♔xb8 c2! 3 ♗xc2 ♔xa6 and Black draws. How can White improve on this sequence?

205) White to play
Smyslov - Oll, Rostov 1993.
Here White noticed that if the black king were to capture the rook, it would be dangerously short of squares, and this gave him the clue for a winning combination. Can you see it?

207) White to play
Marxen - Senff, German League 1995.
White has two strong passed pawns on the kingside, but must deal with the advanced Black pawn on b2. How can he keep Black's threats under control?

206) Black to play
Bruchner - Koch, Berlin 1954.
Black appears to be in trouble. His rook is attacked and so is his knight. However, he turned the tables with a fine tactical sequence. Can you see what he played?

208) White to play
Abramovic - Damljanovic, 'Yugoslavia' 1995.
White is very active, but Black seems to have his weak points well defended. How did White now break through?

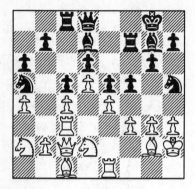

209) Black to play
Hsu - Nunn, Manila 1992.
Here Black found a brilliant
continuation based on drawing
the white king up the board to
its doom in a manner reminis-
cent of the slashing attacks
common in the 19th century.

211) White to play
Westerinen - Sigurjonsson, New
York 1977.
Although White is a piece up
Black has tremendous threats
against his king. How did White
solve his problems in dramatic
fashion?

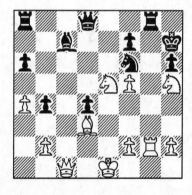

210) White to play
Tarrasch - Consulting Partners,
Naples 1914.
White wants to play 1 ♕b7+,
but Black has 1...♕xb7. Also 1
♖xc5+ is met by the simple reply,1...♖xc5. How did White
brilliantly combine these ideas?

212) White to play
Ribli - Hennings, Leipzig 1973.
Here White found a very powerful continuation which exploited the weaknesses in the
black kingside in dramatic
fashion. How did he continue?

213) White to play
Rodriguez - Spangenberg, Buenos Aires 1995.
In this position White found a clever sequence to exploit the exposed position of the black king. What did he play?

215) White to play
Hracek - Hertneck, Germany 1994.
The black position is full of holes, a fact which White exploited with a clever tactical coup. How did he continue?

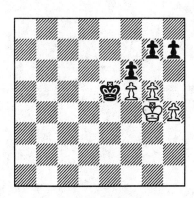

214) White to play
A variation from Chigorin - Tarrasch, Nuremburg 1896.
White had already resigned this game, reasoning that in this position he was certain to lose his f-pawn and with it the game. What did he overlook?

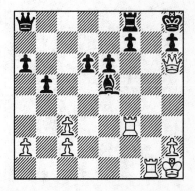

216) White to play
Soultanbeieff - Colle, Antwerp 1926.
The black king is exposed along the g- and h-files but White is currently hampered by the pin against his rook on f3. How did White deal with this problem?

217) White to play
From - Hoi, Vejlby 1976.
White could play 1 ♕xd8+
♔xd8 2 ♘xf7+ and 3 hxg6, but
Black's passed a-pawn would
then prove very dangerous.
How can White do better?

219) White to play
Alekhine - Bogolyubov, World
Championship 1934.
With two good pieces for a
rook, it looks as if Black has the
upper hand here. However,
White's forthcoming sequence
proved that this is not the case.

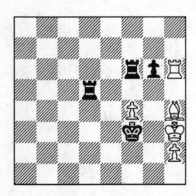

218) Black to play
van der Wiel - van Wely, Brussels 1993.
Here Black found a brilliant
way to exploit the cramped
position of the white king. What
did he play?

220) White to play
A variation from Kasparov -
Short, *Times* World Championship, London, game 7 1993.
Black is trying to relieve the
pressure against his king by exchanging rooks. Will White acquiesce, or can he do better?

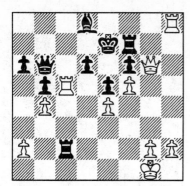

221) White to play
Short - Kasparov, *Times* World
Championship, London, game 6
1993.
Things look bad for White. He
is a piece down, his rook on c5
is pinned and 1 ♕g8 fails to
1...dxc5. Can he survive?

223) White to play
Short - Kasparov, *Times* World
Championship, game 10, 1993.
It looks as if White has a simple
win here with 1 ♘e1 and the d-
pawn queens. However, Kasparov had prepared a clever reply. What did he have in mind?

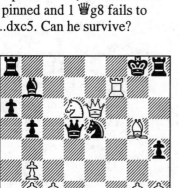

222) White to play
This is a variation from Short -
Kasparov, *Times* World
Championship, game 8 1993.
This is the kind of position at
which a chess computer excels.
White has a forced mate in four
moves. Can you find it?

224) Black to play
This is a variation from Kas-
parov - Short, *Times* World
Championship, game 13, 1993.
Black has a tempting continua-
tion in the form of 1...♘d2+.
Would he be well advised to
take this route?

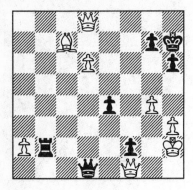

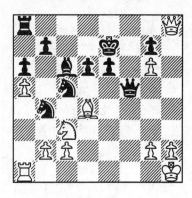

225) White to play
This is a variation from Short - Kasparov, *Times* World Championship, Game 14, 1993. White seems to be in terrible trouble as 1 ♛xd1 is met by 1...f1/♛+ winning. How can he escape from his difficulties?

227) White to play
This is a variation from Anand - Kasparov, Intel World Champ ionship, game 3 1995.
In this position Anand can either grab material with 1 ♛xa8 or attack with 1 ♛xg7+. Which is the best, and why?

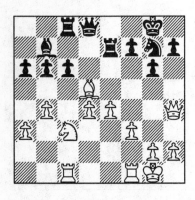

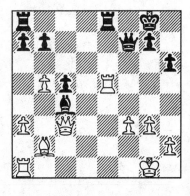

226) Black to play
This is a variation from Kasparov - Short, *Times* World Championship, Game 15, 1993. White has just offered up a piece on d5. What is Black's best reply?

228) White to play
This is a variation from Kasparov - Anand, Intel World Championship, game 4, 1995. This position looks to be heading for a draw. White, however, has a clever tactic which wins material. Can you spot it?

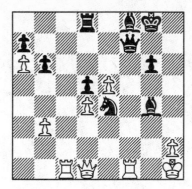

229) White to play
This is a variation from Kasparov - Anand, Intel World Championship, Game 14 1995. White has a tricky decision here as 1 ♕xg4 allows 1...♘f2+ and 1 ♖xf7 allows 1...♗xd1. Which is the best move and why?

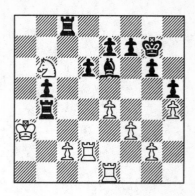

231) Black to play
Anand - Kasparov, Intel World Championship, Game 11 1995. Black seems to be in trouble as both of his rooks are attacked. How did Kasparov, Black to play, demonstrate convincingly that this is not the case?

230) White to play
This is a variation from Kasparov - Anand, Intel World Championship, Game 14 1995. It looks as though Black has got control as 1 ♖g1+ can be met with 1...♖g4. How can White generate play to force a draw?

232) White to play
This position is from a game where I was playing White in a recent simultaneous display. White has good chances to win, as the black pawns are weak and his bishop is restricted. Can you see the winning idea?

233) Black to play
Vetemaa - Shabalov, USSR
1986.
In this position, Black won with
a spectacular move which in-
creased the pressure against
White's queenside to intolerable
limits. What did he play?

235) Black to play
Gines - Trias, Hungary 1995.
This looks like a completely
drawn endgame, but Black
found a way to exploit the constricted position of the white
king. What did he play?

234) Black to play
Ghinda - Gogilea, Rumania
1981.
In this position Black forced a
neat checkmate with a series of
brilliant sacrifices. Can you see
what he played?

236) White to play
Platz - Lampe, Halle 1967.
Black appears to have a solid
wall of pawns around his king
but White's next move exposed
this as an illusion. What did he
play?

237) White to play
Petievich - Castañeda, Russia
1994.
White is a pawn up with a
strong attack and can expect to
win. However, it is always good
to finish off, as White did here,
with a clever combination.

239) Black to play
Seirawan - Lobron, Amsterdam
1983.
Black could capture his opponent's queen with 1...♖xb2, but
this would be a mistake on account of 2 ♖a8+, turning the
tables. What is the best move?

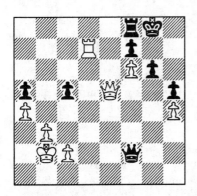

238) White to play
Almasi - Watson, Germany
1995.
Here, White played 1 ♖xf7 (if
Black captures this rook, he is
swiftly mated) and went on to
win. However, he could have
played a stronger first move.

240) White to play
Zukertort - Englisch, London
1883.
In this position White found an
ingenious winning continuation
based on an eventual knight
fork. Can you do as well?

Solutions

201) 1...♗e3! wins, e.g. 2 ♕c1 ♗xc1 3 ♖xc1 ♘xd3 4 cxd3 ♖xd8 winning on material or 2 ♕b1 ♘d1+ 3 ♔h1 ♖f1+ mating.

202) 1 ♗f6! leaves Black without a good move, e.g. 1...♕xe4 2 ♖xg7+ ♔h8 3 ♖g8 mate; 1...♖xf6 2 ♖xg7+ ♔f8 3 ♖g8+ ♔e7 4 ♖1g7+ ♖f7 5 ♕xf5 winning or 1...♕xf6 2 ♖xg7+ ♔h8 3 ♕xh7 is mate. Black tried 1...♕xg4 2 ♕xg4 ♗xf6 3 hxg7 but soon lost.

203) White wins with 1 g4! which leaves Black without a good reply. The trap is 1 ♖d1, which looks good, but fails to the simple 1...h6 when 2 ♖xd5 is met by 2...♖e1 mate.

204) 1 b8=♕ ♗xb8+ 2 ♔b7! and White will eventually queen the a-pawn, e.g. 2...c2 (if Black moves the bishop then 3 a7 will queen) 3 ♗xc2 ♔b5 4 ♗d3+ ♔a5 5 ♔xb8.

205) 1 g4+! ♔xe4 (if Black does not play this, he loses his bishop) 2 ♘f2+ ♔xf4 3 ♖g1! and now 4 ♗d2 mate is coming and if 3...e4 4 ♘h3 mate.

206) 1...♖f3+! 2 ♔xh4 ♘e7 3 g6 (the only move to delay mate) 3...♘xg6+ 4 ♔g5 ♖h6 and mate by 5...♖f5 is unavoidable.

207) 1 ♖b7! b1♕ (if 1...♖xb7 2 e8♕+ ♔g4 3 ♕e2 mate) 2 ♖xb1 ♘xb1 3 g4+! (3 f6 ♔g6 and White gets nowhere) 3...♔xg4 4 f6 and although White is a rook behind, he will play f7 and then queen.

208) 1 ♖xf6! ♖xf6 (if 1...♔xf6 White wins with 2 ♕h6+ ♔xf5 3 ♖e6!) 2 ♕g5+ ♔f7 3 ♖e6! and Black has no good move as 3...♖xe6 loses the queen to 4 dxe6+. Black tried 4...♖xf5 but lost after 4 ♕xf5+ ♔g8 5 ♕g5+ ♔h8 6 ♖e7.

209) 1...♘xg3! 2 ♔xg3 ♕h4+! and now White actually played 3 ♔h2 ♕xe1 and Black soon won. The point of Black's combination is revealed after 3 ♔xh4 f4! (threatening ...♗f6 mate) 4 ♔g5 h6+ 5 ♔xg6 ♖f5! 6 h4 (6 exf5 ♗e8 mate) 6...♖cf8 7 exf5 ♗e8 mate.

210) 1 ♗c7! is decisive, e.g. 1...♖xc7 2 ♖xc5+! ♕xc5 3 ♕b7+ ♔xa5 4 ♖a1 mate or 1...♖xc7 2 ♕b7+! ♖xb7 3 ♖xc5 mate.

211) 1 ♕xg7+! ♔xg7 2 ♗d8+! ♔h8 (2...♔f7 3 ♗h5 and 2...♔h6 ♖h3 are both mate) 3 ♖g8+ ♖xg8 4 ♗f6+ ♖g7 5 ♗xg7+ ♔g8 6 ♗xd4+ ♔f8 7 ♗xb2 with an extra piece.

212) 1 ♖g6! fxg6 2 fxg6+ ♖xg6 3 ♗xg6+ ♔g8 4 ♕xh6 and Black

is losing, e.g. 4...♕e7 5 ♘xf6+ ♕xf6 6 ♕h7+ ♔f8 7 ♘d7 mate.

213) 1 ♕h5! ♗xc6 (otherwise the threats of ♕xf7+ and ♕xh4+ are impossible to deal with) 2 ♕xf7+ ♔d6 3 ♖fd1+ ♗d5 4 ♖xd5+! exd5 5 ♕f6+ ♔c5 6 ♖c1+ and Black collapses.

214) After 1 g6! h6 2 ♔h5! Black cannot capture with 2...♔xf5 as this results in stalemate and he has no other way to improve his position. If instead 1...hxg6 then 2 fxg6 f5+ 3 ♔g5 f4 4 h5 f3 5 h6 gxh6+ 6 ♔xh6 f2 7 g7 f1♕ 8 g8/♕ also results in a draw.

215) 1 ♗h6+! wins, as if 1...♔xh6 2 ♘f7+, 1...♔f6 2 ♘xd7+ ♘xd7 3 ♗xd7 ♕xd7 4 ♗g5+ or, 1...♔g8 2 ♘xd7 ♘xd7 3 ♕e6 mate.

216) 1 ♖g2! and if 1...♕xf3 2 ♕xf8 is mate. Meanwhile, Black is helpless against White's intended 2 ♕xh7+! ♔xh7 3 ♖h3 mate.

217) 1 ♘f5+! gxf5 2 ♕xd8+ ♔xd8 3 h6 and the pawn will queen.

218) 1...g5! wins, e.g. 2 ♗xg5 ♖xh6+ 3 ♗xh6 ♖h5 mate, 2 ♖xf6 g4 mate, or 2 fxg5 ♖xh6 3 gxh6 ♖h5 4 h7 ♔f4 and Black again wins.

219) 1 ♖xd5! cxd5 2 ♖f8+ ♔c7 3 ♖f7+ ♖xf7 4 exf7 and queens.

220) 1 ♖e6! destroys the black position. 1...fxe6 2 fxe6+ wins the black queen, while if 1...♘g8 2 ♕h4+ ♔g7 3 f6+ ♔f8 4 ♖xe8+ ♔xe8 5 ♕g5 and White wins.

221) 1 ♖h7! leads to a perpetual check draw after 1...♖xh7 2 ♕xh7+ as Black's king cannot escape the checks.

222) 1 ♖g7+! ♔xg7 2 ♘f5+ ♔f8 (2...♔h7 3 ♕h6+ and 4 ♕g7 mate) 3 ♕e7+ ♔g8 4 ♕g7 mate.

223) After 1 ♘e1 Black counters with 1...♕g4! threatening mate on d1. Following 2 ♘xb3 ♕xd7! Black is doing very well.

224) No. After 1...♘d2+ 2 ♔g1 ♘xb3 3 ♖xc2 ♘xd4 it looks as if Black has won two pieces for a rook, but White has a sting in the tale - 4 ♖c4 and wins a piece.

225) 1 ♕f8! leaves Black having to be content with a draw, e.g. 1...♕xf1 2 ♕f5+ with perpetual check.

226) 1...cxd5 runs into trouble after 2 ♘xd5 and Black has no good way to continue (e.g. 2...♗xd5 3 ♖xc8 ♕xc8 4 ♕e7 or 2...♖xc1 3 ♘xe7+ ♔f8 4 ♖xc1 ♕xe7 5 ♕xe6+ ♔xe7 6 ♖c7+). However, after 1...♖d7! 2 ♕xd8+ ♖cxd8 Black is assured of a level endgame.

227) 1 ♕xg7+, continuing the attack. If 1 ♕xa8 then 1...♕g4 threatens mate on g2 and attacks the bishop on d4.

228) 1 ♖f5! wins as 1...♕xf5 is met by 2 ♕xg7 mate.

229) 1 ♕xg4! enables White to draw after 1...♘f2+ 2 ♖xf2 ♕xf2 3 ♕xg6+ ♗g7 4 ♖c7! ♕f1+ 5 ♕g1 ♕f3+ 6 ♕g2 with a draw by perpetual as it would be very dangerous for Black to exchange queens.

230) 1 ♗xf6+! ♔xf6 2 ♕h6+ ♔f7 3 ♕xf4 ♕xf4 4 ♖xf4 and the endgame is level and should be drawn.

231) 1...♖xc2! 2 ♖xc2 (2 ♔xb4 ♖xd2) 2...♖b3+ 3 ♔a2 ♖e3+ and Black emerges two pawns ahead with a trivial win.

232) 1 ♘g6! plans to bring the knight to h8 when Black will have to retreat his king to defend the f7-pawn. White then advances his king to attack the b5-pawn. If Black tries 1...fxg6 2 hxg6 ♔e7 then 3 ♔d5 wins as the White b-pawn will cost Black his bishop.

233) 1...♕b5! cannot be captured by either knight or bishop on account of 2...♘b3 mate. White tried 2 ♖d2 to defend b2, but then 2...♘xc3 3 bxc3 (3 ♗xb5 ♘b3 mate) 3...♕b1 mate followed.

234) 1...♖xh2+! 2 ♔xh2 ♗f2+ 3 ♔g2 ♖h2+! 4 ♔xh2 ♕h4+ 5 ♔g2 ♕g3+ 6 ♔h1 ♕h3 mate.

235) 1...♘g4! 2 ♘xg6 ♔f2 forces checkmate, e.g. 3 ♘f4 ♔g1 4 ♘d3 ♔h1 and after the knight moves, 5...♘f2 mate follows.

236) 1 ♕xf6+! ♔xf6 2 ♖f1+ ♔e7 3 ♗g5 mate.

237) 1 ♖d8! ♖xd8 (1...♕xd8 2 ♕g7 mate) 2 ♕f6+ ♔g8 3 ♗c4+! ♕xc4 4 ♕g7 mate. Also full marks for 1 ♖d7 ♕xd7 2 ♕xe5+ ♔g8 3 ♗c4+ with mate to follow.

238) 1 ♕e7! leaves no answer to 2 ♕xf8+! ♔xf8 3 ♖d8 mate.

239) 1...♕xf2+! wins for Black, e.g. 2 ♔xf2 ♖xb2+ wins material, or 2 ♕xf2 ♖xc1+ mating.

240) 1 ♕b5! ♕xb5 2 c8♕+ ♔f7 3 ♕xe6+! ♔xe6 4 ♘c7+ and White emerges a piece up.